Isle Abbots
A Somerset Village
Barbara Rickitt

> Dedicated to the memory of
> Elizabeth Bicknell
> 1911 – 1999
>
> Who inspired me to write this book
> About the village she loved

Self - Published, 2016
Text copyright © 2016 by Barbara Rickitt
Bromes House, Isle Abbots, TA3 6RW

All rights reserved. This book or any portion thereof may not be reproduced or used in any manner whatsoever without the express written permission of the publisher except for the use of brief quotations in a book review

Printed in the United Kingdom by Remous Ltd., Milborne Port DT9 5EP   ISBN 978-1-78280-989-0

~~~ Contents ~~~

Introduction……………………………………………..………………………... 3
Isle Abbots Location……………………………………………………………....4
Early years in Isle Abbots: up to AD1800……………………………………….. 5
Glimpses of Village Life from 1800……………………………………………. 15
The Church: History, Events and Architecture; the Jubilee Room……………... 21
The Isle Abbots Baptist Church/Chapel………………………………………….39
Farming: The Main Farms, the Occupants and Labourers…………………….. 43
Isle Abbots from the Air: 1973…………………………………………………..61
Housing: A Walk around the Village: Houses and some of their Occupants…….63
Education: Schools and the Playgroup………………………………………….. 83
Isle Abbots in the Two World Wars……………………………………………...91
Shopping………………………………………………………………………... 95
Transport……………………………………………………………………….... 99
Special Occasions, Jubilees………………………………………………………. 101
Recreation………………………………………………………………………. 107
The Friendship Club……………………………………………………………. 111
The Village Hall…………………………………………………………………113
Employment Overview…………………………………………………………. 120
Flooding………………………………………………………………………... 121
Bibliography and Acknowledgements …………………………………………. 122

Cover photograph by Interface Aerial - www.interfaceaerial.co.uk

~~~ Introduction ~~~

I have now lived in Bromes House, Isle Abbots for 36 years, and soon after I arrived here, a long-time resident, Mrs. Elizabeth Bicknell, fired my interest in the history of our village in Somerset. In the 1970s Elizabeth produced a slim booklet about the village. This must have taken a lot of research, especially bearing in mind the lack of computers and modern facilities. Over the years she lent me various typed or handwritten findings and I photocopied everything I could to keep for the future. She also kept a village scrapbook of newspaper cuttings and photographs, which she eventually gave to me.

In my earlier years in the village I was busy running a smallholding and looking after a growing family and I now regret that I did not think to record more facts from some of the elderly residents, many of whom were born in the village and lived here all their lives: a mine of information and local anecdotes now sadly lost. However, I decided to start making records of conversations with people in the village to update Elizabeth's book for the Millennium. It is now late 2016 and I am finally putting things together!

I am indebted for Elizabeth's research and for information from other villagers still present, and also some now sadly passed away. I have seen many people come and go and the small changes that happen gradually, but the basic structure of the village has not changed much and history is still in the making. Perhaps someone will update this book in years to come.

I make no apologies for copying portions of Elizabeth's work, particularly about the early days. Her writings were based on ancient records and documents so it seems pointless to try and alter things.

I began with the idea of putting everything into chapters, i.e. church, school etc. but soon realised that up until the late 1800s the church and village were so entwined that everything seemed to present itself as dependent on each other. When it comes to separate chapters there may be some deviation from the chronological history, but at times it is difficult to extract bits without spoiling the flow of Elizabeth's writing.

I realise that despite my best efforts, there may be some inaccuracies and that facts told to me from people's memories could have become slightly dimmed over time. Maybe there are other things that could be included from as yet untapped sources, and inevitably further things will come to light as soon as this work is published. However, I write this in good faith, and even if it is not a perfectly accurate document it will at least give the readers in years to come a flavour of life in the village.

The pictures and documents have been gathered from a wide variety of people and sources for which I am grateful, all of which I have tried to acknowledge at the end of the book; however, for any omissions I apologise in advance.

It has been husband Martin's task to struggle with the finer points of desktop publishing and design, and for his contribution I am also grateful.

I hope the book is a useful record and an enjoyable read.

Barbara Rickitt,
Bromes House, November 2016

~~~ Isle Abbots Location ~~~

Isle Abbots is a small village lying in the heart of Somerset. Approximately 10 miles to the East of Taunton, 6 miles to the West of Langport and 5 miles to the North of Ilminster.

There was an old saying in the village that a man's whereabouts could be traced by the state of his boots. Blue Lias showed he had come from Fivehead, the flints at Ilton cut his boots and the gravel was picked up at Isle Abbots.

The gravel seam runs through the village and just to the east of Otterham Lane is a waterlogged gravel pit. The subsoil is heavy clay.

Collinson in his history on Isle Abbots in 1791 refers to the "strong wet clay" suitable for the growth of oak trees, but few of these remain.

The map shows the parish boundary on the north at the Fivehead River and on the East it is bounded by the River Isle.

The village centre lies to the northeast of the parish; the hamlets of Badbury, Woodlands and Ashford lie to the south.

The Chubbards Cross travellers' caravan site lies just within the parish on the margin of Merryfield Airfield.

Contains OS data © Crown copyright and database right 2016

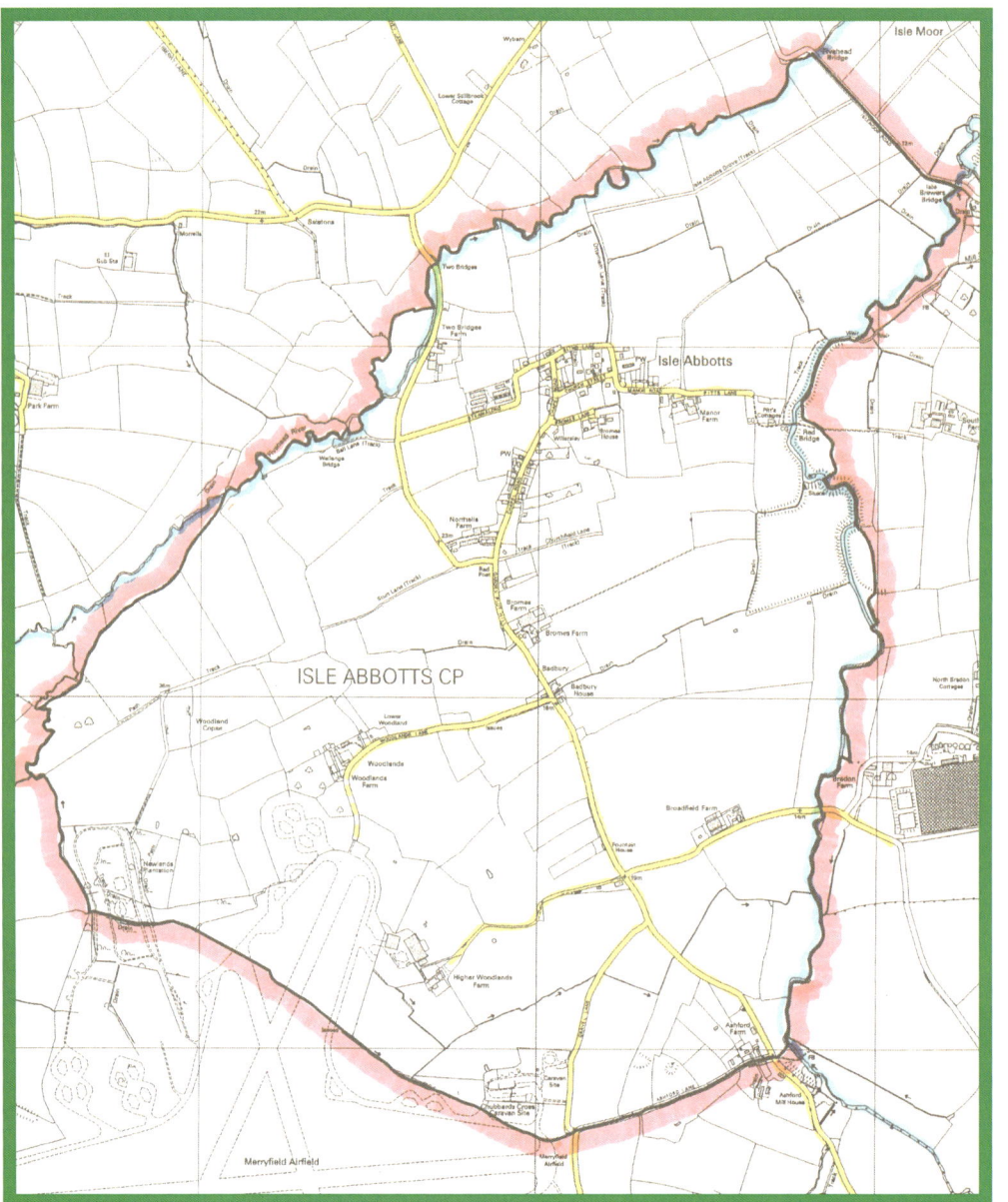

~~~ Early Years in Isle Abbots- up to AD 1800 ~~~

AD 693 – 1400

Ile Abbots, Abbot's Ile, Hyle Abbatis, now signposted Isle Abbots or Isle Abbotts according to which sign you read, are all variations on the name of the village which in the Domesday Book was simply called Ile.

The village grew up close to the river Ile and Abbots was derived from its connection with Muchelney Abbey. Much of the early history is recorded because of its connection with the church and it is difficult to separate one from another at times.

There are doubts as to the founder of Muchelney, but it was established during the reigns of Saxon Kings, probably Ine King of the West Saxons C700 A.D. from whom it received grants of land.

The History of Wessex Charters records this gift of 37 cassates of land on the East bank of the River Isle, on both sides of the Highway, and 3 on the West bank (to Frodi, Abbot of Muchelney) as well as a wood called Stretchmerch. (A cassate is defined as "sufficient land to support a family") This gift was in A.D. 693. In a charter of A.D.792 Kynewolf, King of the West Saxons gave, for the relief of his sins, 8 cassates to Abbot Edwaldo of Muchelney. The land lay between the Earn and the Isle, an exact description of the village today. The Earn is often called The Ragg, but is known now as The Fivehead River.

The next record in A.D.966 from a charter of Edgar King of all Albion may well be a forgery concocted for the purpose of ownership, but nevertheless a detailed description of the village boundaries. These commenced at Ashford, to Claywey to the confluence of the Eorich up the stream to Theoden's field along the stream to the Earn: thence North to the fen, or moor and the stone fortress, down the Earn to the Isle and back to Ashford where there is a field called Clayhanger. In the eighteenth century clay was dug and bricks fired in this field for the rebuilding of a nearby farmhouse. The airfield now obscures the line over the hill down to the streams. The manor thus acquired by Muchelney Abbey was just above sea level on a subsoil of blue Lias clay.

An archaeologist has suggested a Saxon enclave around the Church. Ile Abbots Droveway and Otterham Lane might well date back to Saxon times. The Droveway links up with the Swell Droveway crossing the Ilemoor Road. These droveways linked up with the busy town of Langport whose port took in trade from the Bristol Channel.

In winter Muchelney was only accessible by water. The Fivehead river flows into the River Isle at Bushfurlong, the Isle joins the River Parrett on Thorney Moor and the River Parrett is further increased when the River Yeo joins it south of Langport. So in theory Isle Abbots should have been accessible by water at all times of the year.

By the time the Domesday Book was written in 1087 two tenants had held land for twenty years. Godric paid for 5 hides with land for 2 ploughs. There were 6 slaves, 12 villagers and 5 smallholders. The meadow was 40 acres with 7 acres of pasture. The woodland measured 3 x 1½ leagues. This land supported 25 cattle, 15 pigs, 59 sheep and 1 cob.

Edwin paid tax for 1½ hides with 1½ ploughlands. 3 smallholders had 15 acres. There were 10 acres of meadow; 7 in pasture and woodland measuring 3 x 1 furlongs.

The hide differed in measurement in different shires, the Glastonbury measurement was approximately 120 acres, 8 oxen made a ploughing team. The villagers worked their own land as well as that of their lord; they had some rights of importance as they could not be killed, thrashed or deprived of their land.

The mill that Godric held paid tax of 15/- but its former whereabouts is debatable. Some people think it was on the Fivehead River by some stonewalling, another opinion puts it down by the River Isle at fields called Mell or Millmoor.

The equivalent of the word village was "Tun" an Old English word meaning any enclosed space or group of dwellings. The word survives today in Townfield, one of the common fields. Westfield and Stowey Furlong, now Steamalong were probably also common fields.

Wheat stooks for thatching in Townfield 1981

Temporary cots used by shepherds and swineherds in fields and woods became more permanent homes, which may account for the sprawling shape of the village. Most of the houses were grouped around the church. This was probably a wattle and daub chapel, which the abbey built for its tenants. It may have been burnt down or survived until it was built in stone in the thirteenth century.

In 1239 Bishop Joscelyn of Bath and Wells handed over the Rectories of Fivehead, Chipstable and Ile Abbots to the Abbey of Muchelney. Rectories were owned by Bishops, Lay Lords, Colleges and Monasteries; they grossly neglected their duty of providing Vicars thus accumulating both Rectorial and Vicarial tithes. Also during the last eight years of King John's reign, England was under an Interdict which forbade the administration of all sacraments except Penance and Extreme Unction, so that it was hardly worthwhile presenting a Vicar.

Repeated efforts by the Papacy to remedy this had little effect until the Council of London in 1268, attended by the Cardinals Otto and Ottobonis who were responsible for regulating English Vicarages. Religious Houses holding appropriated churches were to present Vicars and endowments within 6 months or the Diocesan Bishop would do so.

The Vicar thus presented should be 25years of age and a man of good character. Leave of absence from his parish was to be given only for a good reason, such as continuing his studies at University. The Vicar should be provided with a house where he could honourably entertain visitors: his endowment should be sufficient for him to employ a deacon, doorkeeper and 'water-boy' or acolyte. The Vicar had to repair and mend the vestments and to do minor repairs to the chancel. The Abbey of Muchelney followed the Benedictine Rule that did not include the cure of souls; but the Abbot as Rector was responsible for the major repairs of the chancel and greater expenses such as entertaining the Archdeacon.

The first Vicar named on the Ile Abbots list was William de Summer in 1262. Some years later his 'good character' lapsed when he and some friends entered the Manor of Staple and took the goods and chattels of Sir Richard de Briewers.

Ile Abbots was one of the many villages and manors in the forest of Neroche, which extended as far as Earnshill. Immediately on his induction William de Summer received a petition from Sir William Everard, a former Sheriff of Somerset. The Knight prayed that he might have Divine Service celebrated for himself, his wife, his household and his guests in the chapel of his court at Stewley, which tithing, until the 20th century remained part of the Ecclesiastical parish of Ile Abbots. His reasons were the remoteness of his court from the Mother Church of Ile Abbots, the dangers of the ways and the inundations in wintertime. He offered to sustain the proper costs of a chaplain. The Vicar and the Abbot of Muchelney objected to his petition but were overruled by the Bishop of Bath and Wells, William Bitton, the first of that name. The chaplain had to take an oath that he would not take any of the offerings due to the Vicar or Abbot, nor administer the sacraments to any other of the parishioners. On the other hand no Rector or Vicar should claim any gifts made by the faithful for lights, ornaments or books for the chapel. Sir William and his heirs were to pay 12d annually for the privilege. Sir William and his wife Matilda bought land in Stewley in 1248 and 1269.

In the 13th century it was recorded in the Hatch Beauchamp Registers that 'they say there are of the fee of Hyle Abbatis' 5 acres of arable land and 7 acres of meadow, they owe suit to the court of the Abbot of Muchelney at Hyle Abbatis and they owe yearly rent to the Abbot. 'Also they say that the rent of the villains of the same fee is worth by the year 9/1d'. 'Also they say there are of the fee of La Northalls 35 acres of arable land' and '2 acres of meadow'. 'There is of the rent of the villains 16d by the year and they render 1d of yearly rent to Master William of Ditton'. 'The services of the villains of the same fee, as in lifting the meadows and other works to be done are worth by the year 18d and they must do suit to the Hundred of Abedyck'.

Ile Abbots lay in this Hundred usually named as joined to Bulstone: the double Hundred extending from North Curry to Buckland St. Mary. The name of the Ditton family is remembered in Ditton Street in Ilminster.

The names of the free tenants or "villani" of Ile Abbots, as listed in the Exchequer Lay Subsidies are as follows:-

De Willelmo de Ditone	5/-
Thomas de Ile	4/-
Willelmo Havel	2/6
Roberto de Niwant	12d
Willelmo Cotel	2/4
Henrico Body	4/6
Willelmo Cage	3/-
Willelmo Webbe	12d
Johanne le Kyng	3/2
Roberto Tabur	12d
Hugone Cotel	3/-

The currency refers to shillings and pence. This subsidy was paid to the King.

The plague, known as the Black Death, entered the West Country from the port of Melcome Regis in 1347. It lasted three years and decimated one third of the population. This had a major effect on farmland, as stock died and land was untilled. Labourers were scarce so that landowners were forced to pay higher wages.

By 1300 the main body of the church was as we now see it. The five stepped lancet east window sets the tone of the whole building with its plain severity; a deep recess below originally held a hamstone reredos. A few fragments of mediaeval glass reman in other windows. The Piscina and Sedilia present a contrast to each other, the former being elaborately decorated with pinnacled niches which may have held statuettes: the Sedillia consisting of 3 plain tub-shaped stone seats, so perhaps the Abbot could afford to support a Deacon and Subdeacon.

Gregory de Brankescombe was Vicar in 1312 and no other name appears until John de Greton in 1348, which seems a long incumbency. The Episcopal Registers of Bath and Wells are missing for the remainder of this century; but there are lists of clergy whose names appear as having been excommunicated for non-payment of ecclesiastical taxes. If the offender had not paid up within forty days secular aid was sought for his arrest. The name 'Nicholas' of Ile Abbots is on this list in 1381.

The Piscina and Sedelia

AD 1400 - 1600

In 1441 Bishop Stafford instituted John Sperehawk as perpetual vicar of Ile Abbots upon the presentation of the Abbot and Convent of Muchelney. This Vicar was a Fellow of Pembroke College, Cambridge. Among the five Fellows was one Pyke, a co-founder of a chest painted with the College Arms. Within the chest was a sum of £20, which could be borrowed if a sufficient pledge was deposited. John Sperehawk was one of the borrowers when he went with College friends and the Vicar of Tilney to Stourbridge Fair. This great fair lasted for three weeks in September and was the largest in England, attracting traders from Europe as well as from London and the north of England. It took him five years to repay the debt. John Sperehawk left Somerset to become Vicar of Hitchin and died in 1474.

The West Tower of the church was probably completed by 1490, its Perpendicular window resembling those in the extended North aisle.

Drawing by John Buckler, in 1841

The next Vicar of Ile Abbots was Robert Hayne who sat on a commission at "Hacche" Church, which inquired into the Patronage of "Pokington". Ralph Drake was the Cantor at Muchelney Abbey towards whose maintenance the Abbot provided 5 marks yearly from his manor of Camel, 7 gallons of beer and 7 loaves of old bread weekly. He was given a gown and 4 wagonloads of wood from Ile Abbots wood for his stove. Ralph Drakes duties were to attend several services when copes were worn, in the Abbey Church and also to teach four boys and one monk to play the organ and other monks if they so wished.

This may indicate a small school for local boys. There had been a complaint at a visitation of the abbey that the lay organist disturbed the convent though whether this applied to the man or his musical efforts is unclear.

The monks had many recipes for food and drink and a great use for the herbs which we use today; but it is to be hoped that there were not many deaf sufferers in Ile Abbots or they might have had to endure this recommended cure: - 'For to make a man hear that is deaf. Take a great falsen eel unwashed and unskinned and roast him and then take the dropping of him in a saucer and put 3 drops of it when it is cold into the man's ear ere he goes to bed and likewise in the morning 3 or 4 days continually and if he be not a corpulent man it shall make he hear.'

The prosperous days of the Monasteries came to an end when King Henry VIII dissolved them all. In 1539 the last Abbot of Glastonbury was hung on the Tor. The Abbot of Muchelney, Ine or Ivo, was an Ilminster man who by bribery obtained the Abbacy from Thomas Cromwell, though barely of canonical age. The commissioners did not think it worth the trouble of stripping the lead or taking the bells and the stones were gradually absorbed into local buildings. Ile Abbots along with other manors of the Abbey came into the possession of Edward Seymour, Earl of Hertford and his heirs held these properties for the next 50 years.

It was from Sir Edward Seymour in the reign of Queen Elizabeth I that Richard Lamprey received a parcel of land in the village called Whitebarne Pound for himself and his sons John and Henry. The ground measured 5 poles in length, 2 poles in width at the eastern end and 1 pole on the western side, for the yearly rent of 12d and all the customary services. He was also to build a new dwelling place, which later became known as Manor Farm. The Court Role for this concession was dated March 1585. Thomas Isham of Ile Brewers also held copyholds of land "under my Lord of Hertford" in Ile Abbots.

Aerial view of Manor Farm 2006

In 1569 a Muster Role was called and the following able men recruited from the village: -

Hundred of Abdyke, Tithing of Ile Abbotts

John Antony and Henry Bobbet. Pikemen: *Tall men, taking the lead, armed with a 15ft ash pike, carrying a dagger and a slicing sword, and wearing either full armour or an almain rivet, (a type of flexible plate armour).*
Robert Gynnes: Gunner. *Armed with an arquebus, an early muzzle-loaded firearm used in the 15th to 17th centuries.*
Thomas Lumberd, Richard Murleys and Robert Barrett. Billmen: *Armed with a kind of scythe, sword and dagger, wearing an alman rivet and scull (iron) cap.*
Thomas Maundrye and William Tyce: Archers. *Armed with a bow of single or spliced yew 6ft long with quills of grey goose 27in long.*

For bi-monthly practice, shooting butts were built at convenient places. Officers and one J.P. to be present, with no other games to be played that day, not on Sundays.

Those who could not contribute individually combined to provide plate armour, bows and a sheaf of arrows, bills, swords and daggers. Two of these men were John Stower and John Androwe. Until the 20th century the name Lumberd was retained in Lumbard's Plot, the house now called Lumbards. Tyson's was also the name of a house and John Stower may be remembered in Stowey Furlong, now Steamalong.

Lumbards, 1970

There was a means test for the Muster Roll, which affected those owning land worth £5 and under £10. Any person worth £100 whose wife wore silk, velvet, pearls and a chain of gold had to provide a trotter under penalty of £10.

Somerset Wills in Exeter mentioned John Stowre in 1577 and Joanne Tice in 1597 both family names mentioned above

Early wills show bequests made to the Church and village:-

1449   Richard Rumpayn of Ylaabbotes – My body to be buried in the churchyard of the parish church of Ilabbotes to the said church 20/-. To the mending of the bridge of Ilabbotes 3/4d. The residue to Joan my wife and William Rumpayn my son.
1508   Thos Pyper, husbandman of Corry Rivel to the church of Ile Abbots 6/8d
1523   Wiliam Mede of Corymalet 20d
1525   Alexander Buller esq. (Boler?) of Wood. To my olde servant Thomas Lumbard 13/-
1531   Sir Phillip Fulford Knight of Cory Malet to Abbots Ile Church 13/4d

1557   Lady Joan Wadham of Merryfield, Widow, to the church of Abbotes Ile, a noble

By the late 1500's the village of stone built cottages had expanded South and West, with one unusual example of a half-timbered cottage whose wall has long been protected by an outshut, now called Cuff's Orchard.

AD 1600 – 1700

The Revd. Thomas Masters became Vicar in 1593 under the patronage of the Dean and Chapter of Bristol, who had acquired the Patronage after the Dissolution of Muchelney. Masters was born in 1560 and became a Fellow of Merton College, Oxford. He described the Parsonage of Ile Abbots as follows:

"We do present that there is belonging to the Vicarage of Abbot's Ile one little orchard with a garden plot, containing about an acre of land, a little vicarage house, 2 acres of meadow lying in a common meadow called Ilemoor which acres lie in divers places in the said moor in 4 several half acres. We further signify that whereas time exceeding the memory of man there hath been always belong to the Vicar of Abbot's Ile for the time being forty and eight bushels of wheat, twenty and four bushels of oats and 2 cartloads of straw yearly paid out of the Parsonage there, which Parsonage belongeth unto the Cathedral Church of the Undivided Trinity in Bristol and hath always been paid by the farmer or occupier of the said Parsonage until of late it hath been detained by Master Henry Walrond of Lea (Sea of Ilminster) within the County of Somerset and now by Mr William Walrond his son now farmer and occupier of the said Parsonage due to the Vicarage as it doth appear in the Lord Bishop's registry of Bath and Wells by the dispositions of six of the most ancient men of the parish then living and can testify the same. And lastly we present that there is a "pebcvon" of the sum of 6/8d yearly to be paid out of the Vicarage of Fivehead alias Fifett to the Vicar of Abbot's Ile aforesaid at Easter and may appear in the King's Majesty's book in the Exchequer of the valuation of the Vicarage of Abbot's Ile aforesaid".

This terrier was signed in 1613 by the Vicar, Thomas Masters, John Taylor and John Baker, Churchwardens. Henry Oldeforde and William Illett, sidesmen, and E.T.Morgan of Bristol. It seems that the parsonage had long been in secular hands and may have been the house that is now Monks Thatch or it could have been another vicarage house which was on the site of the present Old Vicarage.

The records of the Quarter Sessions interestingly show the problems of various Isle Abbots residents:

Bridgwater - September 1616 - Whereas Roger Baker of Ile Abbotts hath lost by fire £40 and is but a poor man with a wife and 6 poor children; ordered by the court that he do receive £5 from the treasurer of the Hospitals of the Western Division.

Taunton - June/July 1624 – Licence to Robert Backe of Ile Abbotts labourer being a poor man born in the parish, on his humble petition to erect a cottage on the waste of the manor, without 4 acres of land, so as he hath obtained leave & licence of the lord of the manor, & the consent of the inhabitants.

Christopher Lamprey was brought before Sir George Speke and William Walrond on several occasions between 1627 and 1633 for refusing to pay an order for bastardy. This case lingered on as the father excused himself on account of illness and other "impediments". Alice the mother had been allowed to leave the village and the parish was paying for the child. Finally the father gave security to the Churchwardens and Overseers of the poor and the parish was exonerated from all charges on the child. There were other cases of a similar nature.

The Elizabethan Statutes of Artificers laid down detailed rules of Apprenticeships, which prevailed for many hundred of years. The local Justices of the Peace issued the indentures. In 1635 the rules were breached by William Elliott of Ile Abbots, a yeoman, who without licence had made over his apprentice Robert Edwards to William Rowsell of Beercrocombe. Elliott must have been relieved to get rid of his apprentice who was a 'very leud fellow' and had been burned in the hand for felony and burglary. He had been taken on for seven years to learn husbandry, but the court decided that Elliott could be discharged of him.

In 1637 the parish was required by law to repair Steiveleigh Lane (Stewley Lane) described as a highway lying within the parish of Ile Abbots, before the feast of St. John the Baptist next, upon payment of £10.

John Tisse (Tyce, Tyse) was quite wealthy, judging by the inventory of his goods and chattels. He had one bedstead, a feather bed and bolster and two other bedsteads with dust beds. There was another bedstead in the yard with the farming equipment. The total value was £86. He does not seem to have much land; three acres of wheat and one of beans and barley. This would hardly suffice for his nine beasts and one colt, but perhaps he also had rights on the common fields. Some wool was left from his twelve sheep and his one pig would have lived in the cottage garden.

John Perkins inventory in 1637 was even wealthier, leaving two feather beds, two feather bolsters, four feather pillows and a quantity of sheets, blankets, coverlets and table linen. He had about the same amount of land, but many more sheep, leaving twenty pounds of wool. He also left five cwt. of cheese, but only having five kine he may have bought in milk from other farmers. There was a cheesestone and six cheese vats. He left a well bucket and chain. He also had one colt, thirty-one sheep and two pigs. Later when a Window Tax was introduced the cheese room was exempt.

The names of Habberfield, Bromes and Pitt came into view during the 1600's One George Habberfield from Thurloxton whipped a neighbour and called him a lunatic during a quarrel over a sale of land.

In 1624 Laurence Drake, gentleman of Ile Abbots, bought from Sir Francis Seymour and other gentry a house and sixty acres of land including the fields in Ilemoor, Millmoor, Otterham and Ilewood for the sum of £350. His tombstone is in the nave of the Church.

The Bicknell family played a large part in village life. One named Zachary from Cannington had sailed for Weymouth, Massachussets in 1620, probably owing to religious persecution. Twenty years later, two Bicknells from Ile Brewers were named on the Protestation Returns for Somerset. This document was to defend the powers and privileges of Parliament and the Protestant doctrine of the Church of England against Popery and its innovations.

A record of residents during the time when Nicholas Button was the Vicar (1642-1662) states there were 180 names of men and women over 18 years of age, Illetts, Tyses, Viles, Harvards, Pitts. There were so many Pitts that some changed their name to Pytman; the most interesting member of the family being John Pitt of Ashford. It is interesting to note that the current population of the village is about the same number.

John Pytt was a son of Robert & Margaret Pytt who held the land and dwelling house of Ashford Old Farmhouse by deed from Mr Nicolas Wadham of nearby Merrifield. John matriculated at Oxford in 1603 aged 19 and Dorothy Wadham nominated him to a fellowship at her new College of Wadham. He became vicar of Timberscombe, which he resigned upon being presented to the Rectory of South Braden, though it was only a sinecure bringing in £5 per year. When an inventory was made in 1575 William Southeye had held it for twelve years and no service had been held for thirty years. The church at South Braden disappeared many years ago.

Civil War raged and John Pytt lost his many and varied assets and retired to live with his niece Ann at Ilton. His remaining possessions were bequeathed to his many newphews and nieces, his servant Joan Hooper, books to a friend and 20/- to be divided among certain named poor of Ile Abbots. He desired to be buried in the Chancel of Ile Abbots Church, but his tombstone with partially erased inscription still lies in a cottage garden in the village.

The Bromes House date stone

The Brome family lived in the house of that name for over 200 years. The original farmhouse in the village retains its name but the farmlands are now separated from it. The South Porch, which was added to the older building, bears a date stone of 1627 with the initials C.P.S.B. possibly those of Christopher, Phillip and Susanna Brome. (Further details about the Bromes Family and house are in the Farming Chapter).

Members of the Bromes family teamed up with the Walronds of Ile Brewers to persecute Somerset Quakers. John Whiting writing in "Persecution Exposed" described how the Bromes, 'who used to sweep all away', attacked the Friends at Stoke St. Gregory. Phillip Brome was called Lieutenant and Francis was a cornet in Captian Walrond's troop.

Walter Bult was an Ile Abbots Quaker who married Mary Hurford of Marston Magna. Walrond's troop raided Walter Bult's home and drank all his cider, staying at it day and night ' worse than swine'. If the Quakers had sworn to attend the Quaker Session the Bromes would have received 3/4d a piece; but true to their principles the Quakers refused and many were consigned to Ilchester goal. According to Whiting the Bromes helped to devour the Walrond estates as they had done others and many came to 'sad ends'

The Pitt tenement at Ashford was leased to Elizabeth Brome, widow, at this period for a term of ninety-nine years or the lives of her sons, Phillip, John and Alexander. She was probably the Elizabeth Sanders of Fivehead who married a John Brome of Ile Abbots in 1684. The family was distributed through all the surrounding villages.

While the Bromes were sailing out of Bristol making their fortunes in sugar and slaves, four Ile Abbots men joined Monmouth's Rebellion; they were William Mitchell, John Hendy, Edward Burmester and William Grange. They were either killed on Sedgemoor or remained in hiding until James' pardon. In the 19th century there was a mound in the North East corner of the churchyard, which was considered to hold the remains of those who went 'Dooking'. When Thomas Symes was sexton in the early 20th century he found a pit with bones, buttons from a soldier's coat and a bullet. Although the village lies so close to the battlefield there seems to be no other connection with it and the church bells were rung on the accession of King William.

King Charles II had levied a hearth Tax on all houses rateable to the Church or Poor. Ile Abbots had 40 houses taxable. It was of course an unpopular tax and King William abolished it. Phillip Brome had five hearths; Susan Brome, widow, was rated for four. John Perkins for three though one was converted to a stable and one beaten up so he only paid on one. Several hearths were 'beaten up' before the assessor came. The Vicar Robert Pinney was rated for one, the other being beaten up. Most of the cottages had one or two hearths; William Illet got away with one, the other being a private oven and no hearth. This was in 1664-5; the returns were signed by Mr. Henry Drew as sub-collector and John Perkins Tithingman.

Richard Browning was the vicar from 1673-1685. He had the registers re-bound and wrote them in Latin. His family came from Dursley in Gloucestershire. He matriculated at the age of 17 and took his B.A. at Magdalen Hall, Oxford and became vicar the following year. His cottage was opposite Manor Farm where there is now a small orchard and well. It is marked as Brownings on the First Edition of the Ordnance Survey Map published in the early 1800's. Richard's widow was named Catherine and their son Richard was baptised in the church.

The Probate Inventory describes his home and its contents thus-

His wearing apparel valued in the summe of	3. 0. 0.
A bedstead with the furniture thereunto belonging with a little bedstead in the hall chamber two chests and a koffer in the same chamber valued in	5. 0. 0
A bed and bedstead and two pillows in the kitchen chamber	8. 0
In the hall a bed & bedstead with the furniture thereunto belonging, One tableboard one sideboard one trunk 3 chaires in the same room	4 12. 0
His study of books valued in	8. 0. 0
The putur and brasse valued in	4. 0. 0
The sider presse valued in and that belonging to him	2. 0. 0
3 barrells 3 tools 2 hogsides and a halfe hogside, 2 brewing tubs and sitten (salting) tub	14. 0
One sittell one round board 3 chaires one stoole	0. 6. 8
The Fire stuff valued in	0. 6. 0
All forgotten goods valued in	0. 14. 0

(Appraised by) Richard Fowler Rector of Swell
John Collins, Andrew Bullone, Thomas Cozen
(last 3 made their mark)

AD 1700 – 1800

The Churchwardens accounts and more particularly the Monthly Poor Book present an interesting view of life in this century. These books are kept at the Somerset Record Office.

By far the greater numbers of entries are for the killing of vermin, which was a compulsory measure for the protection of corn. Many varieties of birds were killed as well as polecats, hedgehogs and otters. Hedgehogs were supposed to milk cows; this was probably because they may have been found near sleeping cows for warmth, perhaps taking a few drops of milk from a leaking udder. There were plenty of coarse fish in the River Isle for otters; and eels were still being caught in the 20th century with a ball of worsted that entangles the fish's teeth. In 1711 the members of the Parish Church Council decided to allow no more money for catching 'birds & varmints'.

Payments for vermin included:
To Francis Brome – 2 hedgehogs and 2 Jayes	8d
Thomas Harvey – 3 doz & half of sparrows	7d
Nicolas Chick 6 Jayes 3 oops 12 sparrows	11d
John Vile one polecat	4d
William Illott for 6 rats	2d

Several times there was a charge of 1/- for a prayer book; this had to be obtained from a 'paritor', a church official. The Briefs, (national begging letters for disasters) were endorsed in a book costing 2/6d, the paper 1d. Money was laid out for bread and wine at Christmas, Easter and Whitsunday.

There was a ring of five bells in the tower, the Great Bell had to have its 'clipper righted' by Henry Cannicot for the sum of 5/-. To James Baker for his work about the bells 6/9d. William Phillips was paid £1 for 'keeping the clock' washing the surplice and cleaning the churchyard.

Three sacks of lime were bought from Arthur Young and carried to the church for 4/-. Thomas Baker was paid for his work about the porch and limeing it. This parishioner received help towards land improvement. He was allowed 8 bars to repair his enclosure at Otterham and 1.5 lbs of spikes. 2 new posts and four bars for his orchard. But it was not all outgoings; he paid 16/- for an acre in Churchfield.

Mary Baker received a lb. of cheese and a lb. of soap in her illness. James Baker was paid for keeping Mary Chick his sister and cleansing Mary Chick 'she being lowsey'.

Mr Still was paid for bleeding Mary Walrond and providing oils for John Higgins, but there was a charge for going to Langport to see Dr. Michel on account of John Higgins. Evidently the oils were not successful!

After Grace Bullen's funeral her children were provided with meat, cider and wine.
The bell was tolled for most funerals and wool was bought for shrouds. The widow Wiat was given money when she was in need, her husban's coffin was taken up to Stewley, but his corpse was fixed on horseback.

Mr Uttermare was paid 10/- for half a hogshead of cider for John Chick's family. They had Smallpox and were cared for during five weeks; their parents died.

The expenses for Abigail Cox's funeral included liquor, candles, treacle and cheese for the Wakers. Perhaps it is after this lady that the watery depression in the centre of the village is named Cox's Pit. Before it was partially filled in during the 20th century, ducks swam on the pond and the bull was taken to drink there.

Among the needs of the poor money was paid out for taping and welting Edward Jame's shoes and providing him with hedging gloves, 3 napkins for the Bullen children, yards of Brin for shirts, pockets for Dorman's coat and a bushel of wheat, a stay for Bullen's maid, 2 mob caps, 2 yards of Lincey Wolsey and many coats, waistcoats and jackets.

The Poor House was at Woodlands, the most likely building being Woodlands Farmhouse, the earliest part of which could be 16thC. An extension was added on the eastern side in 1736, altering the original three rooms and cross passage building to a rather rambling structure which may have been designed for the welfare of the needy. Philip Harvard put in a new threshold for the Poor House for 6d with shoulder spikes costing 8d. William Adams thatched it for 3/-, three stitches and seven billies of reed cost 3/6d.

Northalls was for many years part of the property of the Pyne estate. Mr. Pyne held a court there as late as 1791, probably in the same building where the Abbot received suit from his tenants. Sir John Beauchamp was assessed for one hide in Ile Abbots, Roger at Cross of Ashford for one virgate (a quarter of a hide) and Thomas de Mony for one virgate in Stewley. Stewley, some five miles to the west, was once part of the parochial parish.

John and Nancy Humphry outside Woodlands Farm in 1999

Northalls Farm, date unknown

The village is approached from the North by a narrow bridge over the Fivehead River known as "Two Bridges" and marks the boundary with Fivehead parish, The date stone just visible above the centre pillar is 1769.

~~~ Glimpses of Village life from 1800 ~~~

Note: Many of the spellings and names in this chapter are taken word for word from original documents. They were written at a time when accurate spelling was less important than it is today. In most cases they have been transcribed unchanged.

By the middle of the 1800's the village had begun to change. People were less dependant on the church, the Baptist Chapel was formed, formal education began, shops and trades were established. So from now on some subjects will have more detailed chapters of their own. In such a small community it is sometimes difficult to disentangle one aspect of history from another, and some subjects might overlap.

In common with many other country villages Isle Abbots reached its peak of population in the mid-1800's with over four hundred residents. Then came the decline in population with the two world wars, the increased mobility offered by railways and motor traffic, and this resulted in the dispersal of many of the older families.

The enclosure of open fields had already begun in Tudor times, and few remained in Isle Abbots by the time the Enclosure Act of 1815 was passed. However, this did affect about 200 acres: Otterham, Millmoor and Ile Abbots Wood. Some of the landholders were bought out but the poorer ones who pastured their cattle on common land or who had a few strips of open field received no compensation. They were doubtless persuaded that their labour would be required to build and maintain the hedges and ditches and that the improved farming methods would lead to more employment.

One of the larger landholders, William Pyne, Lord of the Manor of Northalls, received an acre of land on the edge of one of his holdings but relinquished his right to the soil of the common land in Ile Abbots Wood.

Other landowners mentioned in the Enclosure documents were Charles Brown, Mrs Elizabeth Brome, Henry Humphry, John Walrond, the Still family and the Vicar, the Rev. John Mules (junior), whose Glebe land measured one acre two perches.

Both John Mules and his father, who preceded him in the vicariate, chose to live in Ilminster and were buried there. The son has a memorial tablet in the chancel of Isle Abbots church. It may have been the fact that neither of these vicars lived in the village that prompted William Humphry to write that "few cared about their souls or knew anything of the Gospel", and prompted him to found the Isle Abbots Baptist Church.

The Dissenters had always maintained their place of worship by voluntary contributions; however the Established Churches were financed by Church rates. Hence the rhyme:

> *"We've cheated the parson, we'll cheat him again*
> *For why should the Vicar have one in ten?"*

The Church rates required the tenth sucking pig to be donated to the Church as well as the tenth lamb together with something from every beast on the farm; even the sheep and its wool paid its share. Small gardens were required to pay a penny. The Tithe Communication Act was passed in 1836 to remedy this complicated state of affairs that had existed for many centuries.

When the results of the new rating system were published, every part of the 1877 acres in Ile Abbots was listed with its Owner and Occupier. The land was measured, the cultivation described and each portion rated in money instead of kind. The total rateable sum for the village was £449 6s 0d from which the Vicar received £100 6s 0d and the Dean and Chapter of Bristol £349. There still remained a few unenclosed plots termed 'waste', which were listed as being occupied by the owner.

The Earl of Egremont was the owner of land at Ashford including Ashford Old Farmhouse, which was occupied by the Sawtell family, who farmed about 30 acres. William Baker occupied the remainder of the estate, which included the fields of Woodfalls, Blue Button and Churbers. There were seven enclosures of this name where today travellers occupy the Chubbards Cross caravan site.

Edward Hyder Brown of Shepton Mallet owned the land around Manor Farm (then known as Whitebarne Pound), which was farmed by John Page. Several acres were held in trust for the Hatch Beauchamp Chapel. The fields called Socksoles were in trust for the poor of Honiton. Small parcels of land, mainly in the detached portion of the parish in Stewley were in trust for the poor of Gittisham, Honiton, Ottery St. Mary and Sidbury. A few acres were in trust for Ilminster Grammar School.

Lower Woodlands, known then variously as School Farm or Trotts, was in trust for Langport Grammar School and had been the subject of lawsuits since 1679. The whole property including the house amounted to about 60 acres; among the fields named were Gidlands, Lunders, Summerleaze and Sweethams.

Samuel Humphry farmed at Bromes, which was owned by John Scott Gould, and subsequently by Major Barrett whose family lived at Mordens in North Curry. A date stone, W. B. 1880 is on the barn at Badbury, which has now been converted to a private house.

William Tilley was the occupier of William Pyne's land round Northalls Farmhouse. William Still farmed his own land from Stills Farmhouse next to Northalls.

In 1841 the village was given easier access to the Capital by a coach called 'The Defiance' which called at Ilminster. Its name suggests the many perils that could be faced en route. It left London Piccadilly at 4.30p.m, stopped for supper at Andover and arrived in Ilminster for breakfast before going on to Exeter. The railway soon arrived with the Chard to Taunton via Ilminster line opening in 1866. Hatch Beauchamp was the nearest station to the village until Ilton Halt opened in 1928.

~~~~~~~~~~~~~~~

The 1851 census is particularly interesting in that it shows that of the 320 inhabitants, 194 were born in the village and lived in 68 houses. The formerly prominent names of Bromes and Ilott no longer appeared. Village life centred around the farms; the men were mainly farmers or agricultural workers, their wives glovers or seamstresses. Single females often worked as household servants or as dairymaids. However, in the 1841 census one James Gibbs was listed as a Chemist and Druggist and Richard Patten as a shoemaker.

John Ashton was classed as a landowner and lived at Woodlands where three houses now remain out of the original seven. There were five homes at Roundoak where the thatcher family of Hooper lived. From Badbury northwards all the houses were addressed as 'The Street'. The village was fairly self-supporting even having a staymaker (corset maker) whose husband was a stonemason, as was another member of the Dight family.

At Tysons William Humphry kept an Inn. Two other members of the family kept a grocery store. Abraham Tapp, Master Machinist, lived at Colliers where there was a resident blacksmith. There were two sawyers, another blacksmith, a carpenter and a baker who kept a general store. Alice Burrows who lived at the (original) Old Vicarage was the schoolmistress and her husband William was a tailor. In 1875, William was recorded as being the Parish Clerk. Walrond the butcher lived in a house opposite Marshes. The Baptist Minister, Mr Chapple, lived in the village but not yet at The Manse. He was a widower looked after by a housekeeper. However, there was still no resident vicar.

Samuel Baker was the Waywarden, supervising upkeep of the roads in the Parish. A copy of his receipt book shows payments to R Patten for flints 17/10d, a new rate book 3/6d, various payments to W. Wolmington and other villagers (presumably for work on the roads) and expenses to the Magistrates meeting of 1/6d.

Extract from the disbursments records of Samuel Baker, waywarden for the Parish of Isle Abbots from June 1851

In 1854 a school was built for the education of "children and adults of the labouring, manufacturing and poorer classes of the village". The original school, now the Jubilee Room, was superseded in 1877 when the Board school – the present Village Hall - was built.

A report from The Imperial Gazetteer of England and Wales in 1873 mentions that the manor of Isle Abbots belongs to the Duchy of Cornwall.

~~~~~~~~~~~~~~~~~

A ledger found by Mr T. Channing whose uncle founded a building business in Hatch Beauchamp makes interesting reading. Although lengthy, difficult to read in places and with questionable grammar and spelling, it gives a good insight into the properties in Isle Abbots at the time. It is interesting to note that just a small number of people owned many of the properties. Most were rented out or tied to farm workers.

~~~ 1890 ~~~

Mr E Barrington – Barn and barn floor, chimney piece, parlour ceiling, hearth oven, work on cottage near school, ceiling passages and wash house. Work on W. Woolmingtons cottage and at Mr Barringtons.

Mr Wm. Goodland, I.A cottages at Braden

Mr E Humphry – rep at Mr H Pattens at Two Bridges. Rep walls & granary steps, cementing & stopping round windows, 7 coping stones 4' long.

Mr B Goodland – whitening milk house & pump house

Mr Cotty – rep. plast. Lime wash cottage

Mr Ben Goodland – work at Bad Burry (i.e Badbury) Dairy house

~~~ 1891 ~~~

Mr Heman Patten at Two Bridges – rep. furnace

Mr Ed. Humphry – pitching pig styes at Broad Mills – slate for hearth, 2'6" mantle register, building new chimney at Bad Burry cottage

Mr Robert Tapp – rep. plast & lime wash, fixing hamstone plinth

Mr John Humphry – fixing kitchen grate at Woodlands dairy. 6 firebricks at 1/-

At Manor farm – rep. barn roof – building tank at Hembrys cottage – tiling & paving closet.

To Will Edwards at Ashill – laying old paviour at late Will. Humphry's house at Ile Abbots Pantry, wash hse backdoor yard, recess in kitchen

Goods returned from **Ile Abbotts Baptist School** – 120 chamfered bricks, 250 slats. This work included stone & lime from Rock, 2000 bricks from Hatch hauled by Mr. John Humphry, coal ashes from Mark Adams etc.

~~~ 1892 ~~~

At **Mr Edward Barrington** – rep. plast. & lime washing at late Marshes place.

At **Late Humphrys** – rep wall by gate & piggery shutting & painting Bad Burry Dairy hse & rep.& fixing downlet pipes. 4 men most of 4 days at 12/6d a day. Materials – 3 bag lime 3/6d, 2 loads of coal ashes 3/-, plaster hair 1/-, cement, white lead & 28 lots of paint for gable end & shutting.

Mr E Humphry Woodlands – rep. plast. in bedroom & schoolroom, fixing scullery window. Building chimney for furnace, rep. slates & tiles on roof, rep. drains at Broadfields, rep. plast & lime washing & collaring, tiling closet, 100 building bricks, 5 roman tiles, 25 slates & nails, 4' sheet lead for chimney, 2 10" iron ejects & gratings for drain, 1 bucket of cement, 1. 8" iron eject. etc.

~~~ 1893 ~~~

Mr E Barrington – rep. plast & whitening. Rep. barn floor, rep. plast. & lime washing late Marshes Hse. Plast & lime washing & fixing grate & repairing drains at Garlands cottage at Uttermares. Rep. fireplace & furnace at Barringtons – materials 1 iron black, 1 furnace grate, 1 grate used at cottage. Total £3 3s 6d. made out Nov. paid Feb 1894.

Miss Patten – rep. plast. & whitening, rep. slates at the cottage near Boweys total 16/- made out 1894 & pd 1895.

Mr Hayman – rep. lime washing plast. Bake hse. Kitchen ceiling & pantry, total 5/-

Mr B Bicknell – 12 gallon galvinizing furnace 7/6d. 1 Bath stone 13/-, fixing stone & furnace 2/6d, 12 bricks & mortar 1/-, furnace cover 2/-

Ile Abbotts school board – rep kitchen grate, refixing furnace, rep last. & limewashing back kitchen 7/-.

At **Mr Ben Bicknells**, dr. to Major Barratt. Repairing fence, walls, rep. plast. Outside of dwelling house. Repointing south gable end with Portland cement & painting same with 3 coats of paint.

Mr E Humphry at Woodlands – counter lathing & plastering trap house roof. Repairing tiles on stable roof, repairing walls in barton, repairing in front passage £7.15s.11d.

~~~ 1894 ~~~

To Major Barratt at Mr B Bicknell's. (Bromes) Repairing, plastering, whitening ceiling in kitchen & newly paper walls. Repairing, plastering outside of house, repairing tiles over pumphouse. 3 men one day. Materials 10' deal board 1/6d, mortar whitening 3/-5 pieces of paper.

J. C. Thomas at Cottey's house – repairing, plastering & whitening & fixing grate, one man & apprentice at 10d a day. Digging out tank & building same for new closet paving & tiling same, repairing wall east end of house, repairing chimney & fireplace & tiles back room. Lime & sand & carriage, stone & carriage, paviour, 25 roman tiles, battons & nails & bricks - £2.12.0.

Mr E. Barrington – repairing closet wall & tiles on roof, 6 roman tiles & labour at Davies cottage near the Tapps. Repairing tiles & shutter at Uttermares cottages, repairing tiles at J Paines cottage, whitening ceiling, repairing fireplace at J.Harvey's cottage, repairing wall beside of road by Mr Barringtons, repairing, plastering & lime washing Lumbards cottage.

To Mr. Thomas for contract work at 2 cottages at Ile Abbotts near Mr Barringtons farm, total £1.17.6d.

Further entries are included in the Farming chapter.

In 1894 the first parish meeting was convened in accordance with the Local Government Act. Mr J. Humphry was elected Chairman and Waywarden and Mr. E. Barrington District Councillor under the Langport Rural District Council. The new vicar, the Rev. J. H. Taylor was also present.

~~~ 1900 Onwards ~~~

In 1901 Mr. Hooper tendered a contract to repair the roads around the village for a year until March 1901 for the sum of £58. This was accepted and Isle Abbots entered the 20th Century.

There was a pond at Cox's Corner; traces remain as today's Cox's Pit. Albert Adams who worked at Bromes Farm used it for watering Mr Bicknell's bull and his three carthorses. His wife Nellie's ducks were let out from the shed to swim on the pond. The shed opposite their house in Church Street is still known today as 'The Duck House'.

In 1910 a special Parish Meeting was held to discuss an application to the Postmaster General for the installation of a Telegraph Office at the Post Office. The application stated, "Ile Abbots and neighbourhood are situated in a very isolated position being 4 miles from the nearest Railway station and doctor. The district is a very important agricultural centre occupied chiefly by large farmers by whom the want of a Telegraph Office is greatly felt." The Postmaster General was concerned that not enough business would be generated to cover the expenses of £25 per year, but permission was granted if guarantors for one third of the deficiency could be found. The following then offered to be Guarantors: Messrs E. Barrington, E. Humphry, J. Humphry £1 each, Mr B. Bicknell 15/-, Messrs S. Tapp and J. Perrin 10/- each, Miss Lane and Mr Joshua Crocker 7/6 each, Messrs J. Garland, Job Crocker, R. Dare, B. Goodland and the Vicarage 5/- each. However, it is not recorded if the guarantees were ever required!

After the First World War, a circular was received from the L.R.D.C. concerning houses for the working classes. It was proposed six houses be built, four for labourers at a rent of 2/6d a week and two for artisans at 3/6d. Nearly ten years later no applications had been received and it was not until about 1935 that the first pair were built. Two families from Roundoak moved in, the Adams and Dares; their old cottages were allowed to fall down. These first council houses still exist between Cox's Pit and the Village Hall. Two more were added later.

After World War 2 two more pairs of houses were built behind the church, replacing stone cottages that were pulled down. In one of these had lived Annie Dight who delivered the post in the village. A carrier from Ile Brewers brought the mail as far as Red Bridge and announced his arrival by blowing his horn. Annie also did a vast amount of washing mainly at nighttime. Her mornings were taken up with delivering the post, drinking cups of tea on her round and at the same time collecting washing for her evening job. She softened the hard water by adding "lye water" made from wood ashes. She obviously took pride in her work as the clothes were beautifully ironed.

Red Bridge, 2009

The village footpaths were well used and the stiles were kept in good repair. They were used daily for postal deliveries; farm workers had to lift their bicycles over them. However the footpath known as 'Church Path' between Mr Bicknell's (Bromes House) and the Vicarage seemed to cause the Parish Meeting constant concern as they asked The District Council to keep it in proper order in 1903, then again in 1921, 1939, 1949 & 1953.

The footpath to Fivehead

As mentioned previously, many of the cottages were tied, their occupants moving from one to another depending on which farmer they worked for. Many also housed two families. The old bread ovens started to fall out of use as a baker delivered bread four times a week, a butcher delivered twice a week and the oilman came weekly.

A team of plough horses was still in use after the war at Woodlands although that farm was the first in the area to use a tractor (a three wheeler) early in the century. Mr W. Clarke's father used to drive up to a thousand sheep from Woodlands to Bridgwater Market. Broadfields Farm (now demolished) near Bradon sent oak timbers to be shipped from Bridgwater; on one occasion the horse and cart broke down at Two Bridges Farm.

The L.R.D.C. were asked to make the Ile Abbots drove to Ile Brewers passable for farm traffic as its bad state caused inconvenience to the village; this request was refused. They were then asked to repair the footbridges between Floodlands and Burrows, and between Ile Abbots and Curry Mallet as by doing repairs previously, they had admitted responsibility.

Owners of wells were asked to clean them out and have them regularly inspected. Those at the school and Marshes Farm were especially mentioned.

A joint scheme for a mains water supply was started in 1932-1936 between Langport and Chard. The Ile Abbots branch main came from Barrington through Walrond's Park and through the fields to Bradon and Badbury, then up the road into the village. This was supplemented by a balancing reservoir at Woodlands until 1964 when a new 8-inch pipe was put in from Beercrocombe to Curry Rivel via Two Bridges, the water originating at Combe St. Nicholas where the River Ile has its source.

In 1945 the Parish Meeting discussed the possibilities of a bus service through the village and proposals were made. In due course Hutchings and Corneilius Services of South Petherton provided an infrequent bus service to Taunton.

In 1954 a special meeting was called to discuss the Taunton Postmaster's letter relating to the correct spelling of the village. It was decided that the now recognized spelling of the village is 'Ile Abbots' and the meeting carried this.

In 1955 first mention was made of providing a bus shelter. Mr William Clarke eventually built this in 1959. Surprisingly a plaque on the shelter reads "Queen Elizabeth II Coronation Shelter" It was damaged by a heavy goods vehicle in 2009.

After a few quiet years the RAF Training Command, then flying Vampires and Meteors, reopened the airfield. From 1956-58 766 Squadron flew Sea Venoms whilst Yeovilton runway was being rebuilt. In 1972 the station was renamed H.M.S. Heron of the R.N.A.S. and used as a training base for naval helicopters.

In 1959 the County Education committee offered the now disused school for use as a village hall at £1 per annum rent, provided the village maintained it.

In 1963 the Langport RDC suggested amalgamations between villages and that Isle Abbots should become a ward of Fivehead Parish Council, together with Isle Brewers. It was strongly opposed.

As a result of the 1973 local government reorganisation, the Parish Meeting was elevated to the status of Parish Council under the chairmanship of Squadron Leader John Steele. The Langport Rural District Council was dissolved; the village then came under the jurisdiction of Yeovil District Council, this name changing to South Somerset District Council in 1985.

The landscape around the village changed when Dutch Elm disease struck in 1973. As a result, the rookeries moved house to the alders and withies at Two Bridges. Many replacement trees were planted, some with donations given for the Queen's Silver Jubilee. Towards the end of the 1990s more tree planting took place and members of the Parish Council planted daffodils on many of the verges.

In 1980 the divisional surveyor was taking a close look at the floods at Two Bridges in view of producing a major scheme. The village is still waiting!

In 1981 the Parish Council was invited to appoint a Civil Defence Officer who would attend courses and advise parishioners on Nuclear Defence.

● Isle Abbotts Parish Council chairman, Sqd-Ldr John Steele (left), and warden of St Mary the Virgin Church, Col John Stevens, and the offending electricity pole, which spoils the view of the historic church tower.

Eyesore pole sparks row
Local newspaper, 25/2/1987

In 1990 the Parish Council decided that an application should be made to the District Council for Conservation Area Status. This was granted for the centre of the village.

In 1993 main drainage was laid though the village and most properties were connected. After much campaigning the power distribution authority placed their supply cables underground in the vicinity of the church and British Telecom promised to do the same with their lines at a later date.

On 21 November 1994 The Parish Council Minute Book was completed after 100 years. Present at this meeting were Squadron Leader John Steele, Mrs Evelyn Stevens, Martin Rickitt, Anthony Habberfield and Leonard Harden. A new book was started

The Chairmen of Isle Abbots Parish Meeting/Council have been:

John Humphry	1894
Rev J H Taylor	1896
Edward Barrington	1897
John Humphry	1897
John Henry Humphry	1924
Arthur Gray	1959
John Steele	1969
Richard Humphry	1994
John Steele	1995
Anthony Habberfield	1997

Because of the Second World War there were no entries in the minute book for the years 1940 to 1944.

Towards the end of the 20th century some old barns had been converted to houses and a few new bungalows built.

However, the village, with no through road, can still be described in the words of the Daily Mail reporter of 1907 as being "five miles from anywhere".

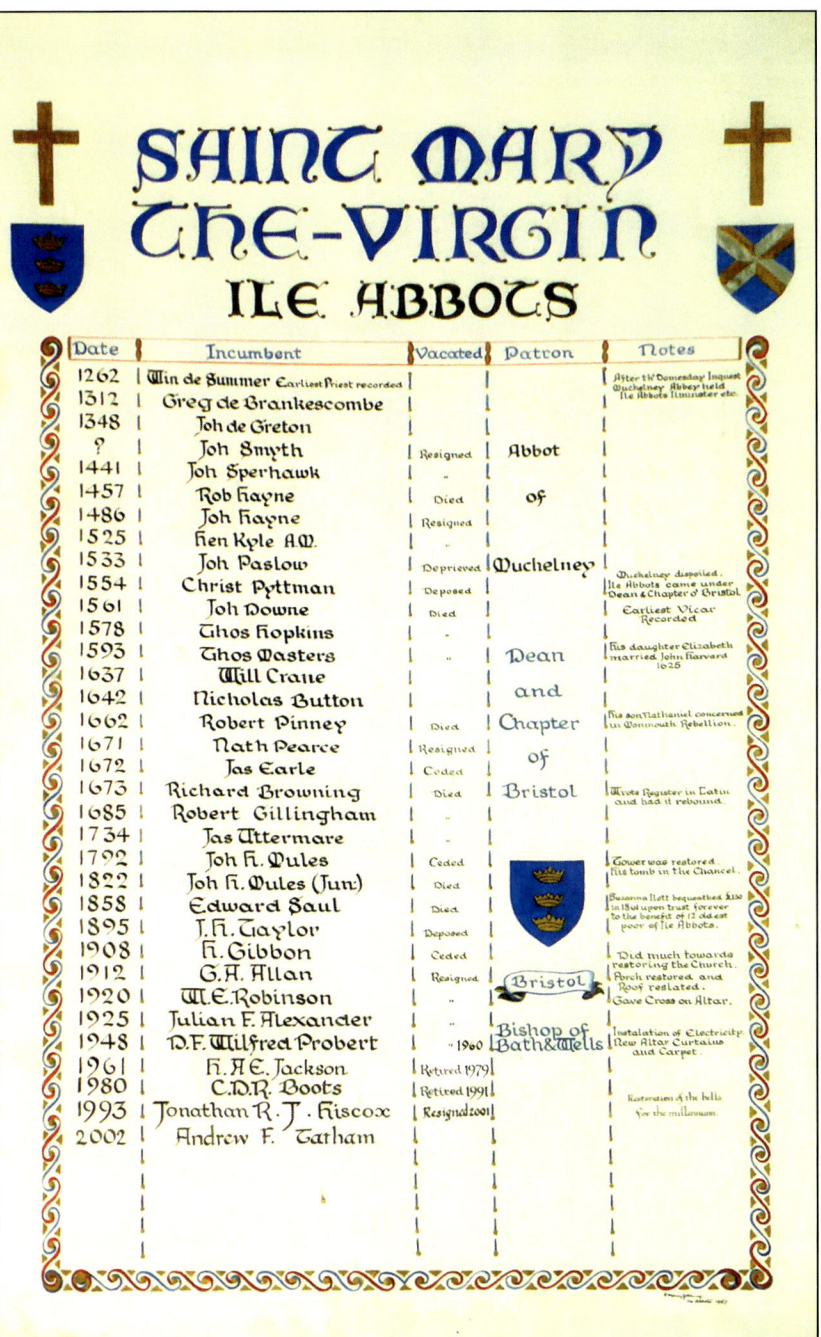

~~~ The Church ~~~
History, Events and Architecture

SAINT MARY THE VIRGIN ILE ABBOTS, SOMERSET

Built by the Monks of Muchelney,
  Long before the Reformation,
Was Saint Mary's of Ile Abbots,
  A church of rare fascination.
Its age has never been determined,
  Which is most regrettable.
The tower is one of the finest,
  It is unforgettable.
The statues, tower and doorway
  In perfect harmony merging,
All dedicated to Saint Mary,
  The Blessed, Sacred Virgin.
Go you to this moorland church,
  Enter it and pray,
Tender you an offering
  Ere you go away.

Unknown source

From a copy of 'Church Briefs' between the years of 1653 and 1717, it would appear that despite being mainly a farming community, the people of Isle Abbots were very generous towards others in need.

A house-to-house collection in 1653 raised £1 12s 3d towards the relief of the town of Marlborough which was consumed by fire and about 224 dwellings were destroyed.

When this report ended in 1717 there appears to have been about 118 collections for other churches or towns, mainly suffering from effects of fire.

Perhaps the generosity of the people of the village has an effect on the feelings felt by Pevsner in his report on the church's history –

"On entering through the south doorway one is at once transported into an atmosphere of great purity and lucidity."

~~~~~~~

THE VICARAGE. There does seem to be some confusion as to which buildings were designated as the vicarage. Rev. Thomas Masters who became vicar in 1593 gave a lengthy description of his vicarage previously mentioned in the first chapter of this book. Some thought it might have been the cottage now called Monks Thatch.

The Rev. Richard Browning who was vicar from 1673-1685 lived in a cottage marked as Brownings on the First Edition of the Ordnance Survey Map, opposite Manor Farm.

In notes made by a Mrs. Wood of Isle Abbots in the 1950s she states the following: "Parsons Cottage was pulled down about the year 1894 and the new vicarage, coach-house and stable built thereon". It would appear that this was most likely located on the land now occupied by the present Old Vicarage. Rev. Wilfred Probert was the last vicar to reside in this vicarage before it was sold for private use.

Also over the years the vicar of Isle Abbots has sometimes lived in a vicarage at Isle Brewers, so it seems there was a lot of changing around. When Rev. Jackson was vicar of Isle Abbots, he also looked after Ilton and lived in the vicarage there.

Then came Rev. Roy Boots and a new house was built for him in Ilton, by which time he had charge of Isle Brewers and Hambridge as well.

By the time Rev. Jonathan Hiscox arrived there were seven parishes to care for, Ashill, Horton, Broadway, Donyatt, Ilton, Isle Brewers and Isle Abbots. The parish of Hambridge had been transferred to Kingsbury. The vicarage at Broadway was then used and the one at Ilton sold.

Rev. Andrew Tatham followed and also lived at Broadway. Before he retired in 2014 the parish of Hambridge was once again joined to the benefice.

~~~~~~~

When Rev. Edward Saul was appointed vicar in 1858 he came to a church that had not had a resident vicar since Rev. John Mules had been appointed in 1792. John Mules was also vicar of Ilminster and master of the Grammar School there. He had served as a curate in Broadway, and vicar of Muchelney.

In 1822, his son, Rev. John Hawkes Mules, followed him. He became vicar of Isle Abbots, Kingstone and Ilminster. With so many souls to administer to, Isle Abbots church building and its worshippers did not receive much attention.

It would appear that in the three years Rev. Saul was vicar he was not a happy man as his obituary stated that 'he was a vicar who lived alone, died alone and was buried alone'. However, he deserved credit for starting the restoration work on a much-neglected church.

~~~~~~~

THE BURIAL IN WOOLEN ACT: This Act began in 1666 and was in force until 1814, although not repealed by statute until 1863. It required the dead, except Plague victims, to be buried in pure English woollen shrouds. It was required that an affidavit be sworn in front of a Justice of the Peace (usually by a relative or credible person) confirming burial in wool, with the punishment of a fine of £5 for non compliance. Parish registers were marked A or Aff against burial entries to confirm this, or marked "naked" for those too poor.

The purpose of this act was to protect the glut of home produced wool and to help lessen the imports of foreign linen, although it was often ignored. In 1678 it was extended to also line coffins in wool.

There remains a small torn piece of printed-paper showing an affidavit –

Hannah Dodridge and *Mary Hill* being two credible perſons, do feverally make Oath and ſay, that the Body of *Mary Govier* late of the Pariſh of …..*St Mary Magdalen* in the ſaid County of Somerſet, deceaſed, was interred in the common Burial Ground, adjoining and belonging to the Parish *of Abotts Isle* on the 23rd Day of *May 1863* and that the ſaid Body was not put in, wrapped or wound up, or buried, in any Shirt, Shift, Sheet, or Shroud, made or mingled with Flax, Hemp, Silk, Hair, Gold, or Silver, or in any other Thing than what is made of Sheep's Wool only, nor in any Coffin lined or faced with any Cloth, Stuff, or any other Thing whatſover, made or mingled with Flax, Hemp, Silk, Hair, Gold, or Silver, or any other Material or Thing whatſover, but Sheep's Wool.

In 1854 the first village school was formed and put in the care of the church. (See the Education chapter). The building was still under the care of the church when it became the parish room in 1878 but was then neglected until Lady Anna Gore-Langton financed its repairs in the Jubilee year of 1887. It was restored again by the Rev. Gibbon and again by his successor the Rev. Allan.

Around this time the rare barrel organ was installed in the church. (Further details are given later in this chapter). This replaced the musicians' gallery where the serpentine and bass viol were played and the gallery unaccountably disappeared, along with the church clock.

In 1861, S. Illot bequeathed £150 upon trust forever for the 12 oldest poor in Isle Abbots, to be administered by the church. The church continued to distribute this money until 1994 but the amount of interest each year was very small and it became somewhat embarrassing to establish who the 12 oldest or poor were in the village. With the permission of the Charity Commissioners this trust was dissolved and the remaining money put into church funds.

In 1855 the church received a Form of Prayer and Thanksgiving, printed by the printers to the Queen's most Excellent Majesty. This was to be used throughout the country at morning and evening Service after the General Thanksgiving: "To Almighty God for the Signal and repeated Successes obtained by the Troops of Her Majesty, and by those of Her Allies, in the Crimea; and especially for the Capture of the Town of Sebastopol." There followed a long and somewhat pious prayer.

Again on 31st January 1900, churches were requested to say prayers on behalf of Her Majesty's naval and military forces now in South Africa.

In 1891 a Rev. F. Birch was appointed curate at £120 per annum to reside at Fivehead. Then in 1893 Rev. J. Langley was licensed as a curate at £100 per annum to reside in Ilminster. When Rev. Langley left he was presented with a clock from the grateful congregation. The presentation letter read "We the undersigned parishioners of Isle Abbotts, while asking your acceptance of the accompanying time-piece as a small token of the high esteem in which we have held you, heartily thank you for the kindness you have shown during the time you have been among us. We trust that God's blessing may follow you in your new sphere of labour and while we regret your leaving us we hope our loss will be other's gain." *Signed by 80 parishioners.*

The Rev. J. H. Taylor was an unfortunate vicar who made the headlines when he intended to conduct a marriage service in the parish church. The bridegroom was Mr. A. J. Burt and the bride Miss Emily Hooper.

The Daily Mail reporter gave an account of the disastrous service on September 2nd 1907:

"The church was full when the vicar beckoned the groom and best man to the chancel step. The vicar was told that the bride had not arrived so he walked about the church. When she duly arrived the party assembled at the chancel steps. Mr. Taylor started the service. Luckily the bridegroom heard him mutter 'I commit these people to the ground, earth to earth' The bride, not unnaturally, started to weep and her aunt rose up and advised the vicar that he was reading the wrong service; he tried again and said 'I baptise thee with water'. This caused turmoil among the congregation; the vicar after several vain attempts on different subjects retired and sat down"

The bridegroom asked a friend to go to Ilminster for another clergyman and a lady offered to cycle to Ilton for the Archdeacon. Meanwhile the vicar and the bridegroom had an argument in the churchyard, the vicar eventually throwing down his surplice. After some time the Archdeacon came and conducted the marriage service, followed later by the clergyman from Ilminster. The seventy people in the church dispersed, the bride's uncle who had a wooden leg, stumping indignantly up and down the church.

The Rev. Taylor with his long white beard and pony trap left the village having been defrocked by the Bishop. It is believed that he had a drink problem but at the Diocesan hearing the poor man described how he had suffered sunstroke returning from South Africa, his daughter had died which had preyed upon his mind. He had considerable financial worries over the building of the new vicarage, which had caused depression, and for 2 or 3 months he had not had 2 consecutive hours' sleep. He also suffered from an internal complaint. He had asked to be buried at Ile Abbots but there is no record of this.

The congregation had dwindled during his vicariate; it took two further vicars to increase the congregation again.

CHURCH REPAIRS 1874-1911

In 1874 Lady Anna Gore-Langton of Hatch Beauchamp extensively restored the tower in memory of her husband. It was at this time that the clock and musicians gallery were removed.

By 1900 the church was in a bad state of repair. It would appear that the beautiful North Aisle was in a state of collapse. It had been built without proper foundations and owing to the absence of sand; mere clay had been used for mortar. This had made everything weak and no drains existed to carry off surface water, the windows began to fall apart when the ground became saturated and the rafter ends began to decay. In 1908 under the Rev. Gibbon permission was sought to allow the following repairs:

- To underpin the North Aisle and South Porch, resetting the stones and windows.
- To underpin the walls of the Chancel to a depth of four feet.
- To rebuild the East gable from the level of the springing of the window head, raise the East window and provide a new gable cross.
- To relay the open channel round the walls on a bed of concrete.
- To strip the roof, remove the plaster ceiling, repair the timbers, relay the slating on new battens and re-plaster the ceiling.
- To repair the plaster on the walls and expose the stone quoins to the windows.
- To take up the paving of the floors and relay the paving on a bed of cement concrete altering the position of the kneeling step and provide a new altar rail and footpace.
- To repair the glazing and casements and provide additional ironwork to the windows.
- To provide new Chancel seats.
- To lower the pulpit and rearrange its surroundings.
- To slightly move the Chancel screen.
- To move the two seats on the North East of the Nave and re erect them in the North Aisle to the east of the North Door.
- To move the font a few feet
- To put up new lights and also build a low pressure heating apparatus for warming the church.
- To move the organ to the North Aisle.
- To move the pavement and monumental slabs first putting on the memorial slab to Catherine Browne an inscription showing from whence it has been moved.
- To put vestry cupboards and safe.
- To open up the rood loft stairs.
- To remove the deal seats in the North Aisle, and put a wood block floor under all the seats.
- To remove the nave roof ornaments and to fill up with concrete all vaults under the church.
- To carefully take up any bodies which may be met with in carrying out the work and decently re-interring them in some other part of the churchyard.

This vast amount of work was undertaken by Messrs. Cornish and Gaymer builders and completed under the leadership of Rev. Gibbon between 1908 and 1911. The repairs amounted to £1,172. 9s. 7d., collected from various sources. The Rev. Gibbon was living in Isle Brewers at the time and spent much time walking to Isle Abbots across the fields that were often flooded.

The architect was Mr. W. D. Caroe of London. In Mr. Caroe's letter of November 1908 he says, "A good deal of repair is necessary to the church but I deprecate any drastic measures to rebuilding, such as I understand have been proposed. They are entirely unnecessary and uncalled for." (Thank goodness for Mr. Caroe's wise words – Ed.)

Major Church Repairs, 1908-1911

Also a report in The Church Builder of 1908 says about Ile Abbots Church "Remote in situation, yet in an archipelago of churches, and within a ten-mile radius of Taunton, this building is of singular beauty, and has escaped, and will continue to escape so far as those at present dealing with it are concerned, many destructive experiences of more prominent parishes."

This report lists all the major features in the church and lists the ten remaining figures in their niches on the tower. Two lower figures are missing. West are figures of The risen Christ stepping from his sarcophagus as in Sodoma's famous fresco in Siena, The Blessed Virgin with Bambino, quite Byzantine in manner St. Peter, St. Paul. East are St. John Baptist and St. Clement of Rome. South is St. George, wonderfully mounted on his quaint charger, with cap on head, showing

Major Church repairs 1908 - 1911

the removal of his helmet; St. Catherine of Alexandria, St. Margaret of Scotland. North is St. Michael with a star for his sole armour.

A photograph in this report shows texts and a shield painted on the walls; these have since been plastered over. It also shows a text in very large lettering over the rood screen reading *'Let the People Praise thee O God'*. There is no record of what happened to this.

Sometime during this period of restoration a stone sarcophagus was dug up and now sits in the chancel.

THE HATCHMENT is of the Stuart House and it is thought that it may have originally filled the chancel arch at one time. Later (according to ancient churchwardens' accounts) it was nailed over the little North door, and there are many entries in the account book about "repairing the Hatchment". What remains is now nailed on the South wall of the tower – it consists of six pieces of wood nailed as horizontal strips. The second strip, counting from top to bottom, is wrongly placed. It ought to be above the right-hand end of the strip. (Journal of the Somersetshire Archaeological Society). The Royal arms shown are said to include those of France.

Thomas Symes who was the Sexton between 1905-10 found buttons off a soldier's coat and a bullet when turning over a mound in the churchyard; also human remains piled one on another as laid in a pit. It was believed at the time that these could have been soldiers involved in the Monmouth Rebellion. During World War One it was found impossible to darken the church windows for the evening service during the winter months. Permission was sought from the Bishop of Bath and Wells to use the church room. This was granted on 22nd September 1917. "To the said George Alexander Allan the Incumbent of the said Parish and to his licensed Curate or Curates for the time being and to all and singular the Parishioners and Inhabitants of the said Parish to assemble in the said Schoolroom for the purpose of joining in the public offices of our Holy Religion."

After the war a meeting was called about erecting a war memorial – "Notice is hereby given that a Vestry meeting will be held in Isle Abbots Church on May 27th 1919 at 8 0'clock in the evening to consider the proposal to erect a brass tablet in the church as a memorial of those from the Parish who had fallen in the late war. To approve the proposed design and position of the tablet, to authorise the Vicar and Churchwardens to apply for a Faculty for the erection of the same".

Signed – Geo. Alex. Allan, Vicar, Henry J. Tapp and E. J. Barrington, *Churchwardens*

This was duly agreed and the tablet is in place inside the church on the north wall. It was paid for by public subscription and there still exists a list of all those who subscribed, ranging from 10d to £5. The total collected was £64.2s.11d.

Celebrations - maybe after the restoration

Rev. Allan wrote by hand a little booklet about the history of the structure of the church, as he knew it. Amongst these papers is a little snippet of paper about a fair:

"According to local tradition a fair was held annually in September. Whatever it was formerly, it became a pleasure fair and was held in the field adjoining the Lamb Inn (now done away with). On the Monday the men rang peals on the bells, and on Tuesday the women. Its origin is unknown and its disuse within living memory (1920)"

When Rev. Allan retired in 1920 he was presented with a silver cream jug and sugar castor.

~~~~~~~~

It is interesting that the church was heated by a boiler that was housed in a pit on the north side of the tower. The structure still remains but has now been sealed up. A bill to the church dated March 1919 from George Small and Sons Ltd. of Taunton, lists deliveries of Coke and Anthracite Nuts amounting to £4.4.10.

~~~~~~~~

Next followed Rev. W. E. Robinson. When he resigned he left a list of instructions for the next Vicar about what he did at different services. On Sundays there was a service of Holy Communion at 7.30am, Matins 11am (except on the 1st Sunday when 10.15). The Catechism for children at 2.30pm, Evensong at 6.30pm. 1st Sunday the Holy Communion at 11am has been sung. I have usually observed the 1st Evensong of a Festival with sung Evensong.

He said: "The Crucifix is my property and may be returned to me if no longer required. It was from Oberammagau. The side Altar is mine and may be returned if no longer needed. It is an old Field Service one used in the war.

In the old doorway to the Rood loft we have had a Christmas Crib, I cannot leave the figures as they were only lent. It should be put on record that Mr. Caroe the architect who restored the church admitted to me that the stone wall at the base of the Screen is a mistake. There is no choir, which I find an advantage. Certain young people meet on Fridays for music practice. I found the Stamp system useful for Sunday morning attendance for children."

These notes give a very good picture of church life in the 1920s.

UNION OF BENEFICES. Historically the Parish of Isle Abbots included various detached outposts, so the parish boundaries were sensibly redrawn. This necessitated legal applications and a report in The London Gazette on 23rd August gave a report on the proceedings at the Court at Buckingham Palace the 15th day of August 1929.

The document is very long and wordy. There seems to be some confusion over who lived in which vicarage (Parsonage House) at what time.

An extract reads: -

"We, the Ecclesiastical Commissioners for England, acting in pursuance of the Union of Benefices Measure, 1923, have prepared, and now humbly lay before Your Majesty in Council, the following Scheme for effecting the union of the Benefice (being a Vicarage) of Isle Abbots and the Benefice (being a Vicarage) of Isle Brewers, both of which Benefices are situate in the County of Somerset and in the Diocese of Bath and Wells. etc. etc.

And ….That upon the said union taking effect the Parsonage House at present belonging to the said Benefice of Isle Brewers shall become and be the house of residence for the Incumbent of the United Benefice.

And …. That with consent of Reverend Morgan John Griffiths, now incumbent of the said Benefice of Ashill, upon the union taking effect all that detached portion of the said Parish of Isle Abbots situate within the area of the Civil Parish of Ashill and containing 'Stewley Farm' 'Radigan Farm' 'Forest Farm' 'Folly Farm' ' Stewley Lodge' 'Wood Cottage' and part of 'Kenny' shall be transferred for all ecclesiastical purposes to the said Parish of Ashill.

And …. The Benefice of Bradon, upon the union taking effect, shall be transferred for all ecclesiastical purposes to the said Parish of Isle Brewers.

On the First of October 1939, at the beginning of World War 2, a printed Form of Prayer to Almighty God was issued: 'This Time of War' to be used in all churches.

Then at the end of the war in 1945 an order of service for 'Thanksgiving For Victory' was issued.

SALE FOR CHURCH ORGAN REPAIRS. A newspaper report reads: "On Wednesday August 15th 1945 (VJ Day) a sale was held in the church room. Tea was served in the vicarage, as the weather was too unsettled and windy to hold the whole affair in the garden as had been hoped. A very excellent tea was organised by the Misses Willcox and helpers. The stalls brought in the sum of £37. 9s. 1d., and several very generous gifts of money were received making a total of over £58, considerably more than the amount required for the organ repairs.

On Friday evening the Social Committee organised a small dance in the schoolroom. Mr. and Mrs. Bert Adams played and Mr. Bernard Habberfield was in charge of the door. The profit of £1.7s. was handed over to the Welcome Home Fund.

CHURCH CLEANING. A handwritten list of cleaning instructions of unknown date is very interesting. "Lamps to be cleaned, filled, attended to for winter services …every week seats to be brushed out, whole of church including vestry swept and dusted … At festivals hangings at both communion tables to be taken down and shaken … Spring cleaning to be done between Easter and Whit Sunday … Special attention needed behind radiators … Church room to be kept clean every week" etc., etc.

Payment: – The cleaner to receive £5 a year for the work. Spring-cleaning: 10/- extra when Council satisfied with work. Three months notice on either side to terminate engagement. At spring-cleaning the windows and high places to be brushed down by men at charge of council.

During the vicariate of the Rev. Probert from 1948 to 1960 electricity was installed in the church and the furnishings renewed. From the accounts of 1948 it looks as if the installation of electricity to the church and church room cost £134.

Rev. D.W.F. Probert vicar 1948-60

The Parochial Church Council Secretary, Monica Dare, wrote a letter of appeal on 20th April 1948 to the Society for Promoting Christian Knowledge. She was asking for a grant for new prayer books, she says, "…You will appreciate that it is useless to ask people to come to the church services unless they first have the services explained to them and they are given a book to use. At present we have very few prayer books and these are mildewed with age and not really fit to be handled."

The vicar's wife Mrs Sonia Probert was very supportive of all church affairs and continued the work of the Mothers' Union, which had been started by Mrs Alexander, wife of Rev. Alexander in 1936 with 13 members. A great achievement was the banner made by expert needlewomen in Eastbourne. The members funded the total expenses and it was a proud occasion when 3 members carried their banner in the Deanery Festival Service at Wells Cathedral.

A newspaper article in June 1959 reports "Wednesday 26th February was a red-letter day for this little branch, when its Banner was dedicated in the beautiful church by the vicar, the Reverend D. F. W. Probert. Members from the Branches at Staple Fitzpaine and Stoke St. Mary, with their Enrolling Members, were also present to take their share in the joyous occasion. For many years this small branch had longed to possess its own Banner, and to take its place in the Banner Procession at the Deanery Festival Service".

The really touching part of the story is that under the leadership of Mrs. Probert, the whole cost of the Banner was covered by personal gifts from members past and present (and a few others) in loving memory of their own mothers, many of whom have already passed from sight, thus forging a link with the unseen.

At the close of the service, Ile Abbots members entertained the visiting Branches to a really delicious finger supper in the church room. "Now Thank we all our God" was sung as an act of praise.

When Rev. Probert retired, the Mothers' Union held a farewell meeting in the church room when Mrs Probert was presented with a beautiful leather handbag and a bunch of Lilies of the Valley on behalf of the members. Mrs. Probert felt very sad at leaving the parish when she had spent so many happy years, especially among the members of the Mothers' Union.

Mrs. Probert used to light the fire in the church room before it was used and also cut the grass on the banks either side of the church path with hand shears. She also took her turn at playing the organ along with Mrs. Eleanor Wood.

With 6 children to keep Rev. Probert had to run a little business as an agent for a farm supplier to make ends meet. He would go around the farms on his motorbike.

Rev. Probert was the last vicar to live in the Rev. Taylor's vicarage, and it was then sold privately. When Rev. Probert died in 1976 he returned to Isle Abbots to be buried just outside the south door.

On 7th April 1960 the Parochial Church Council passed a resolution about the next vicar. "That the need of the parish is for a young energetic priest with moderate Catholic views"

~~~~~~~~~~~~

The Rev. Jackson followed. He had hoped to restore the bell frames but despite a letter of appeal to the village in 1965 this was beyond the means of the parish. However, he did have the heating system installed. He wrote many letters and held fund raising events to enable repairs to the church roof to be made. He arranged loans of £500 each from the Diocesan Board of Finance and the Historic Churches Trust. These were to be paid back at £100 each per year. In 1967 he wrote to the DBF to ask if the repayments could be reduced to £50 per year.

One paragraph of his letter quotes "You might comment that the PCC should not have undertaken these loans unless they could see their way towards honouring their obligations upon the terms agreed in the first case. That could easily have been done, but in the meantime what about the Fabric of the Church? We were told that the work was urgent and that in a few years time, if things had been left, the roof would have fallen in and the pinnacles fallen further into decay. Once that stage had been reached then rapid deterioration would have taken place and before long a ruin would not be far off".

In 1966 the church had held a floral and produce show towards funds. Events were held in the church, the parish room and the school. Another flower festival was held in 1976 with stalls in the garden of Monks Orchard and refreshments at Abbots Orchard.

Mrs. Jackson was well loved in the parish and kept a Sunday school whilst living in the vicarage at Ilton. She was noted for her flower arrangements, being the first to popularise flower festivals in the district. The Rev. Jackson retired in 1979 and Mrs Jackson died later that year.

Their son Bernard organised and financed a permanent memorial to his mother Annie Matilda Eliza Jackson that was dedicated by The Right Reverend E.B. Henderson, D.S.C., D.D. on 27th June 1981. This memorial came in three parts. The painting is probably after the school of Correggio of the Virgin and Child with Saint John the Baptist known as the Madonna of the Goldfinch. It forms the reredos to the altar in the Lady Chapel, a field altar from the First World War.

The frontal was designed and worked by the Royal School of Needlework. It shows the armorial bearings of the Lady Margaret Beaufort, a descendent of Edward III and mother of Henry VII. She owned the Manor of Langport and is traditionally associated with the building of the north aisle.

The memorial tablet on the north wall is of Anstrude Jaune stone and designed by Mr. Kenneth Wiltshire. It was carved by Mr. Douglas Garland at Chichester Cathedral and follows the form of the medieval consecration panels in the east wall of the chancel. During the service the singing was led by the choir of the Chapel Royal of Saint Peter ad Vincula within Her Majesty's Tower of London under the direction of the Master of Music, Mr. John Williams. The ladies of the Parish provided the flowers and provided a tea after the service.

The next incumbent was the Rev. Roy Boots who lived in a new vicarage at Ilton and served the combined parishes of Isle Abbots, Ilton, Isle Brewers and Hambridge. His wife Maureen was also supportive of church events.

In 1982 the rare Barrel Organ was restored (see separate section).

Many fund raising events were held during his time in the village. In September 1982 a 'Rustic Fayre' was organised in the centre of the village. This was very popular and raised well over £1200. There were lots of stalls and sideshows, tractor and crane rides, bygones exhibition, dancing, a dog show, a band and various refreshments including a popular bar run by Colonel John Stevens.

● A cheque for £1,200 is presented from the Isle Abbotts Vintage Fayre, by Bernard Habberfield, of Northalls Farm, to the Rev Roy Boots, for the Isle Parish Church tower restoration fund. Also pictured are Wendy Richards and Len Harden (organisers) and Pat Harden (treasurer).

Bernard Habberfield(left), and son Tony view his threshing machine at the Rustic Fayre

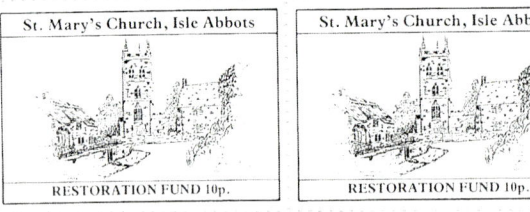

Similar events in fields belonging to Northalls Farm were held in 1984, 1986 and 1987.

Special stamps were printed in 1986, which could be used on letters along with official stamps in the post. These were sold for 10p each in aid of the church restoration fund.

The next vicar was Rev. Jonathan Hiscox who moved into the vicarage at Broadway in 1993 to take over 7 parishes after a big reshuffle and an interregnum of two years when the churchwardens arranged for visiting preachers. He was to be part of an 'Ilminster Team' covering 18 churches under the leadership of Rev. John Reed, vicar of Ilminster.

During Rev. Hiscox's time the church bells were restored and they welcomed in the next Millenium. (See separate section on the church bells)

To welcome the NEW MILLENNIUM on 1st January 2000, a joint service with Isle Abbots Baptist Church was held in the Parish Church. Rev. Hiscox led this service, together with the Baptist pastor, Mrs Joyce Butler.

Just after the bells were restored, the church architect highlighted priority repairs to the north aisle stonework and its pinnacles, along with the tower parapet. The work to the north aisle was carried out at a cost of approximately £31,000.

Joan Crisp, organist for 40 years

In 2001 Mrs Joan Crisp retired as church organist after playing for over 40 years. The PCC held a lunch party at Friars Field, home of Marjorie and Paul Stevens and presented Joan with a basket of flowers. Joan continued to attend services until she became ill and died in 2008 aged 94.

After that time there were visiting organists and later a compact disc player was used with a large selection of recorded hymns together with new matching hymn books.

~~~~~~~~~~~~~~~~

In 2001 a church guide was printed with the help of 'hunky punk' expert Mr. Peter Poyntz-Wright. He also gave a fundraising tour around the church looking at the architecture, followed by strawberries and cream. Later that year he held another talk and slide show in the village hall.

At the Queen's Golden Jubilee Thanksgiving service on 2nd June 2002, Mr. George Withers sang a song that he had written especially for the service –

SAINT MARY'S BELLS
Based on the inscriptions on the bells of St. Mary the Virgin

No one recalls when they last were rung,
Through countless years we've held our tongue;
No living man has heard our call
    ORA PRO NOBIS SANCTE PAUL
    SAINT PAUL, ORA PRO NOBIS
A century we've hung at rest:
A pigeon's roost, a jackdaw's nest.
Our bellropes 'wait the ringers' hands;
    ORA PRO NOBIS SANCTE JOHANES
    SAINT JOHN ORA PRO NOBIS
Then people in the congregation
Felt the need for celebration,
Rehung us and went on to get
A sixth bell to complete the set.
    DRAW NEAR TO GOD
Now, in the tower again we swing;
Over the fields our voices ring.
The moors and villages hear us tell
The glory of Saint Mary's bells
  I WILL NOT FAIL TO SING MY PART ACCORDING UNTO MUSIC ART
  WITH MY SIDE MATES I DO AGREE IN PERFECT SHAPE AND HARMONY

The Leylandii trees on the north perimeter of the churchyard were originally planted as a hedge. However they were neglected, grew into tall trees and started blocking the daylight to the adjoining cottages. In 2004/2005 they were cut down and a new hedge of mixed native species was planted with the help of the playgroup children. This has grown to be very attractive.

The Playgroup "helping" to plant the new church hedge 2005

~~~~~~~~~~

CHURCH TOWER AND RESTORATION 2004 to 2007

After a quinquennial inspection showed up severe cracks in the tower parapets, it was deemed necessary to have these repaired. The church is a grade I listed building, so after consultation with English Heritage and an archaeological survey in 2004 they insisted that much more extensive work than originally planned should be undertaken. English Heritage were able to offer a £50,000 grant towards the work of repairing the parapet, carving and erecting the missing intermediate pinnacles, repairing all statues and their niches, and smaller pinnacles. Cleaning and re-pointing was necessary for the whole tower. Their proposed grant was supposed to cover 50% of the total cost which was a huge sum for the village to find. During the work and further inspection it was found necessary to fix bracing to the tower parapet, and together with other additional work the final sum increased to around £130,000.

This huge undertaking was met by grants from English Heritage, the Friends of Somerset Churches, The Chase Charity and other grant bodies which the church treasurer, Peter Cottel, worked tirelessly to find. The remainder came from extensive fund raising within the village.

The whole of the tower was shrouded in scaffolding for many months and during restoration some of the statues were removed from their niches and traces of the original medieval paint was found on them. The detail that remained after the lichen had been cleaned off was quite amazing. The four newly carved pinnacles were attached by drilling steel rods into the base of the old ones.

Drilling for steel rods to fit the new pinnacles

The excellent team from Strachey and Strachey painstakingly undertook all the renovations. Our church architect, Mr. Bob Chambers and buildings archaeologist, Jerry Sampson, supervised it. Churchwardens Anthony Habberfield and Barbara Rickitt oversaw the work.

The tower displays eight unusual Hunky Punks, the name coming from the old English "Hunkers" meaning squatting on the haunches and "Punchy" which means short legged.

A thanksgiving service for the tower restoration was held on Sunday 2nd September 2007, and Peter, Bishop of Taunton, dedicated the tower. The village choir sang and afterwards refreshments were served in the church. It was a happy occasion for all those involved.

~~~~~~~~

Special services are always held at Christmas, Easter and Harvest when the ladies of

Sally Strachey, Conservator, examining a hunky punk before restoration

Dedication service for tower restoration, 2/9/2007: Bishop of Taunton; Rev Andrew Tatham; Barbara Rickitt & Anthony Habberfield, Churchwardens

the flower team decorate the church beautifully. Singing from the Isle Abbots Choir often adds to the enjoyment of these services. In recent years we have marked the farming year with special services.

Helen Snell, site manager, restoring St. George

In January there is Plough Sunday when an old plough and a milk churn is brought into the church and seeds for the year are blessed. Then in May Rogation Sunday service is held with communion by the Fivehead River to bless the crops, animals and the fields. In August the ancient festival of Lamas is celebrated to mark the first grain of the harvest when bread is brought to church and enjoyed with butter, cheese and jam. Then comes the traditional Harvest Festival at which gifts are brought and auctioned and the money given away. The church and village hall committee alternate providing a harvest lunch or supper each year.

Sadly, the ancient Horse Chestnut tree in the churchyard had to be felled in 2009. It had been looking unhappy for a while and a specialist tree inspector was called in. His visit resulted in the tree being diagnosed with bleeding canker and in a highly dangerous condition. Although everyone was sorry to see it go at the time, the view of the tower and across the fields was much improved.

There are many fund raising events held to support the ongoing upkeep of the church and to restore the church room (see separate chapter). Events have

Georgie Murphy - 1996 Flower Festival

Rev Andrew Tatham blesses the flagpole assisted by John Lucas

Col. John & Mrs Evelyn Stevens

Lunch party at Abbots Orchard to mark the leaving of Barbara Wright, 1990

raised thousands of pounds and also provided a lot of fun for the community. Events have included summer lunches, cheese and wine parties, open tower evenings with Morris dancing and refreshments, sponsored bike rides, flower festivals, harvest lunches, musical concerts and open gardens. Some have featured rides on the railway at Bromes House. A Valentines dinner and the very popular 'full English Breakfast' held several times a year at the village hall are just some of the many enjoyable gatherings.

The church has been enhanced by many memorial gifts over the years. More recent ones being floodlighting the tower and providing new Churchwardens Staves, both purchased with donations from the family and friends of Richard Humphry of Manor Farm who died in 1993.

A new red vicar's cope with matching chalice veil and burse were purchased with donations made in memory of Bernard Habberfield who died in 1999.

The family and friends of Sqn. Ldr. John Steele who died in 2001 gave a flagpole. The flagpole was dedicated at a special service for St George's Day on 25th April 2004. A marquee was also donated to the village in memory of John and erected in the garden of the Old Vicarage where a lunch was served. The band of RNAS Yeovilton provided entertainment.

The family of Barbara Wright gave a seat in the churchyard in her memory. Barbara had been Churchwarden for many years before retiring to Hampshire to be near her family. Barbara was a driving force in the church and can be remembered for instigating 'lively discussions' at PCC meetings and encouraging others to get involved. She died in 2005 aged 92. At her funeral service her daughter said "Barbara's Isle Abbots days were her happiest."

Many people have supported the church over the years whose dedication has kept the splendid building in good repair and active for worship and quiet contemplation. There have been far too many people to mention by name, but one very active couple were Col. John and Evelyn Stevens who left the village in 1995.

The old lamp over the gateway that was donated some years ago by Derold Page was wired up for electricity in 2012 with a small plaque in memory of Mrs. Georgie Murphy who died in 2009.

Steps were constructed either side of the church gate in 2014 to enable easier access to the churchyard. The family and friends of Dafydd Rhys Watts who died in 2013 built them. Dafydd is buried in the churchyard in view of the Old Vicarage where he lived for much of his childhood.

With 8 churches to conduct services in, the incumbents have been assisted by many retired ministers, readers and lay helpers. Rev Andrew Tatham retired in October 2014 and Rev, Philip Denison was inducted in September 2016.

Wells Cathedral: Tim Gibson's ordination as Deacon, 29/6/2014

The church has been priviledged to welcome the assistance of Tim Gibson in a non-stipendiary capacity. Tim was ordained in Wells Cathedral in 2014 and a party of supporters from Isle Abbots attended the service.

More details of the church architecture can be found in the Guide available in the Church.

THE JUBILEE ROOM

The Jubilee Room prior to restoration commencing

The original school given in the care of the Church has been used for many things over the years. For example Sunday Schools, church meetings, whist drives, parties and a library. Having not been used for many years this building was used for a history exhibition for the Queen's Golden Jubilee in 2002. Many villagers were enthusiastic to get this room into use again. It is now known as the Jubilee Room after the Queen's Golden Jubilee and for the fact that it also underwent repairs in 1887 the Golden Jubilee of Queen Victoria. It is now under-going restoration and modernisation as and when funds and manpower allow.

Elaine Guest and team laying the new concrete floor in the Jubilee Room

THE CHURCH BELLS

In May 1996 the project to restore the church bells was begun by churchwardens Anthony Habberfield and Barbara Rickitt with Walter Ashford as appeals chairman and who later took over from Mrs Rickitt as churchwarden. It was a daunting task but there was a warm response from the village and together with generous grants, the necessary funds were raised.

Advice suggested that a new treble bell should be added to the five existing bells. After an inspection by English Heritage it was decreed that the re-leading of the tower roof was necessary before installing a new steel bell frame and re-hanging the bells. The old wooden bell frame has been retained and raised on steel girders to the top of the tower. Work also included new flooring in the ringing chamber, soundproofing, repairs to the stone steps in the tower and installation of electricity to the tower.

In January 1999 four of the existing bells were removed and restored by Eayre and Smith Ltd of Derby. The small treble 15th Century bell was sent for welding to Soundwell of London and the new Treble was purchased from Holland. All the bells were returned to the church by September that year and blessed by the then vicar, Rev. Jonathan Hiscox.

GOING UP: The church bells at Isle Abbots are ready to be raised into position.
Newspaper report, September 1999

The first ringing team, 1999:
Elaine Guest, Walter Ashford, Lois Parsons, John Lucas, John Steele, Linda Welch.

Mr Ashford took lessons in bell ringing at South Petherton Church and then gathered a band of enthusiastic people in the village to learn 'the ropes' in time for the dedication service, taken by The Right Revered Jim Thompson, Bishop of Bath and Wells on 14th November 1999. Refreshments in the village hall followed this happy service.

The bells were restored just in time to ring in the next Millennium. Since then a band of ringers have rung for most of the church services. When Mr Ashford moved from the village John Lucas took over as Tower Captain.

There have been many visiting ringers, the first full peal being rung in February 2001. This consisted of 5,040 changes of Cambridge Surprise Minor in two hours and 53 minutes. On one of his visits to Manor Farm H.R.H. Prince Charles visited the church and inspected the newly installed bells.

HRH Prince Charles tries his hand at bell ringing

The ringers are self-supporting and hold fund raising events making donations to the upkeep of the church fabric.

THE INDIVIDUAL BELLS

Bell No.1. A new Treble cast by Koninklijke Eijsbouts in 1999 inscribed with the names of Revd. J. Hiscox our Vicar, A. Habberfield and W. Ashford, Churchwardens.

Bell No.2. Cast in 1662 by Thomas Purdue of Closworth, near Yeovil. It weighs 7cwt. and is decorated with a vine border.

Bell No.3. Cast in Bristol in the 15th Century and bears the inscription "Sancte Johanes ora pro nabias" It weighs 8cwt. and has a unique initial mark in the form of a Catherine wheel.

Bell No.4. Dated 1633 and weighs 9cwt. It has the following lines inscribed on it: "I will not fayle to sing mi part accordin unto musick arte, with me side mates I do agree, in perfect shape and harmony". It was cast by Richard I and William III Purdue.

Bell No.5. Weighs 11 cwt and bears the inscription: "Sancte Paule ora pro nobis". It was cast c1450 in Bristol.

Bell No.6. Cast in 1619 by Geo. Purdue of Taunton. It is inscribed "Draw neare to God".

THE CHURCH BARREL ORGAN

The rare barrel organ in the church was built by Henry Bryceson of London about 1835 and was among many supplied to country churches between 1820 and 1860, spanning the interval between the age of live music and the advent of church organs.

When it was played for Sunday School, the oldest boy in the class was allowed to turn the handle for the bellows.

It is not known when the barrel organ arrived in Isle Abbots, or whether it was purchased by the church or as a gift. Singing to the barrel organ means quite literally joining in the music of 175 years ago! It most probably had a more decorative front on it when first built. Originally there were 3 barrels with 10 tunes on each and a fourth was supplied through a Bristol music dealer, thus providing 40 tunes, several rather dull chants and a selection of metrical psalm tunes.

Despite its modest size, the barrel organ, with its four stops and ninety-seven pipes, takes advantage of the favourable acoustics at Isle Abbots and provides an ample body of sound.

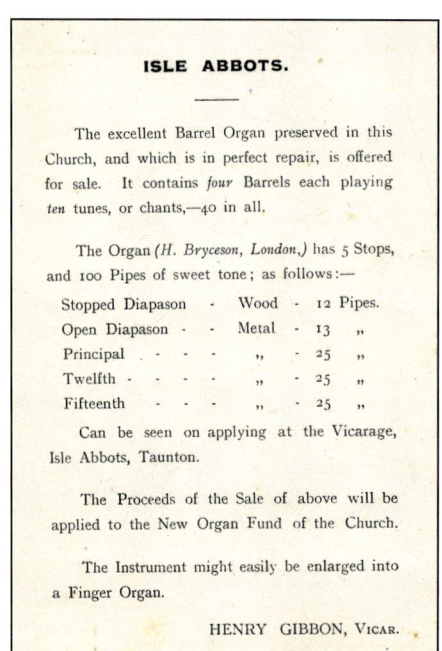

ISLE ABBOTS.

The excellent Barrel Organ preserved in this Church, and which is in perfect repair, is offered for sale. It contains *four* Barrels each playing *ten* tunes, or chants,—40 in all.

The Organ (H. Bryceson, London,) has 5 Stops, and 100 Pipes of sweet tone; as follows:—

Stopped Diapason	-	Wood	-	12 Pipes.
Open Diapason	-	-	Metal	-	13 "
Principal	-	-	-	"	- 25 "
Twelfth	-	-	-	"	- 25 "
Fifteenth	-	-	-	"	- 25 "

Can be seen on applying at the Vicarage, Isle Abbots, Taunton.

The Proceeds of the Sale of above will be applied to the New Organ Fund of the Church.

The Instrument might easily be enlarged into a Finger Organ.

HENRY GIBBON, Vicar.

It is lucky that the barrel organ is still in the church as 2 attempts have been made to sell it. Firstly, it was advertised by Rev Henry Gibbon, the vicar from 1908-1912 with the aim of providing money towards a new organ. Then again in 1975, when the PCC decided it was deteriorating in the damp church, it was decided it could be sold to raise money for general repairs. Fortunately the Diocese refused to give permission and eventually it was taken away and completely restored in 1982 by John Budgen from Ipswich at a cost of £700. This was made possible by a generous donation by The Pilgrim Trust.

The newly restored organ was first on show to the public at a fund raising 'Rustic Fayre' in the village in September 1982. Although not used to provide music for services the organ is still enjoyed when demonstrated at special events.

Simon Jay demonstrates the barrel organ at a church tower open evening, July 2007

Isle Abbots Baptist Church

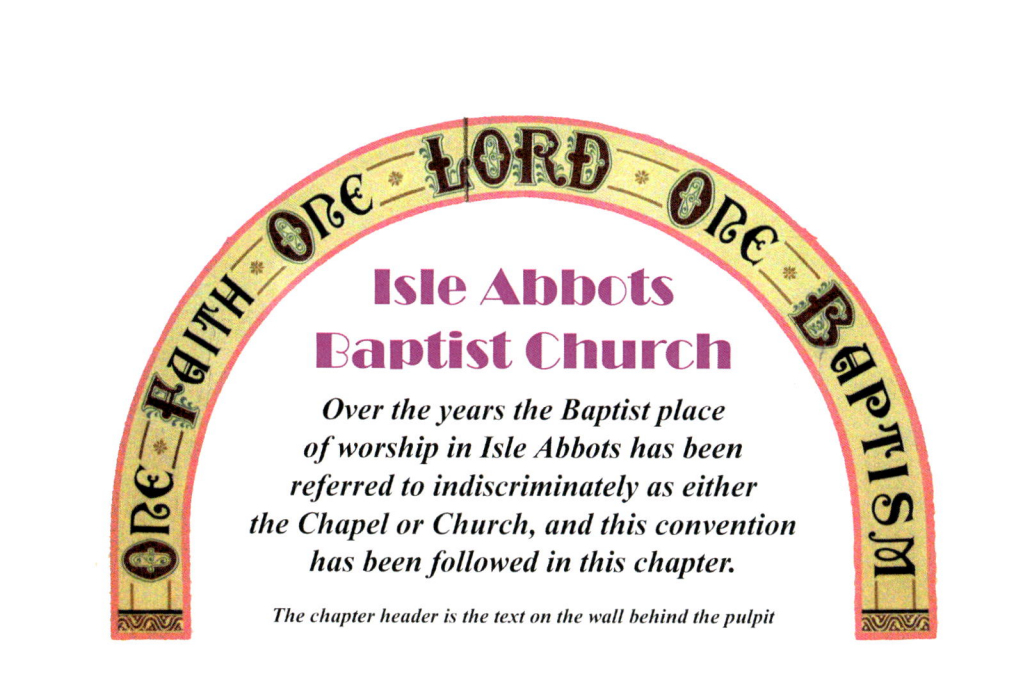

*One Faith * One Lord * One Baptism*

Over the years the Baptist place of worship in Isle Abbots has been referred to indiscriminately as either the Chapel or Church, and this convention has been followed in this chapter.

The chapter header is the text on the wall behind the pulpit

In 1698 the house of Robert Smith in Fivehead was certified as a Dissenters Place of Worship (from C. of E.). Any non-conformists in Isle Abbots at the time probably worshiped with the residents of Curry Mallet, who in 1690 registered the home of Jerome Day, or perhaps by 1753 in the home of Martha Chick at Isle Brewers. Or by 1760 Samuel Burford's house in Ilton.

THE BEGINNING AT ISLE ABBOTS

About 1798, wrote William Humphry, few in Isle Abbots cared about their souls or knew anything of the gospel.

He had attended the Independent Chapel at South Petherton under the Rev. Richard Herdsman for about four years. He felt the urge to preach to his friends and neighbours in Isle Abbots. His nervousness gave way as repeatedly the words came to him "If thou hold they peace, the stones will cry out against thee". He began by reading a chapter of the Bible, praying and singing a hymn. His little congregation grew, and he began to add preaching to his services. He speaks of some persecution and of Prayer Meetings; of the young children of his own and his friends' families, and of the impending problem of baptism. Gradually his thoughts turned to Believers' Baptism. William Humphry therefore approached the Rev. T. Tombs of Chard, who on November 25th 1806 baptised William in the river at Welinge Bridge. (Welinge was on the other side of the road from Stemalong, Isle Abbots).

The following spring William Baker and his wife Elizabeth (nee Humphry) were convinced of their duty and William Humphry baptised them at the same place. "It was supposed", he wrote, "a thousand people were present". Soon after this Susanna Crocker, Sarah Vile and Prudence How were also baptised. They had been Wesleyan Methodists.

On 23rd June 1808 the 6 Baptised were formed into a church meeting in Walronds House Isle Abbots and William Humphry was acknowledged as their teacher.

In the County Record Office in Taunton there is the application to the Lord Bishop of Bath & Wells dated June 20th 1809. "We those names underwritten request that the house of William Crocker (or hogers house) in the parish of Isle Abbots in the County of Somerset, and the Diocese of Bath and Wells may be Registered for the worship of Almighty God according to the custom of protestant Dissenters, agreeable to the Act of the 1st of Wm. and Mary C.18".

The application is signed by William Crocker, Philip Coat Brome, William Baker, Thomas Baker, Henry Humphry, James Humphry and William Humphry, Teacher. Certificate granted 3rd July 1809.

In 1817 another certificate was issued for a Meeting House, (the present chapel) for use of Protestants on the application of William Humphry.

By that time the membership had grown to 13 but during that year and the next

Mrs. Joyce Butler outside the Chapel, June 2002

- 39 -

William lost his mother Hannah, and his dearly loved first wife, Mary (nee Brome), who in 21 years had borne him twelve children. Three years later he married Betsy, the widow of William Crocker and in 1833 they were "dismissed" to the church at Croscombe, which had called William to be their Pastor. He died on 14th May 1835 and was buried in the chapel at Isle Abbots. A man of courage and an earnest evangelist, William Humphry kept the church records assiduously in a good hand.

The Chapel, a 1930's postcard

The Registers show that marriages could be held at the Chapel. The document signed by James Frederic Horatio Warren, the Superintendent Registrar of the District of Langport certifies that the building named the Baptist Chapel in the Parish of Isle Abbots having been duly certified as a place of Public Religious Worship was registered for the Solemnisation of Marriages therein, on 19th March 1847.

By 1850 the membership had risen to 53. Mr John Chappell took over as Pastor in that year and in his 22 years of ministry added ten pages to the records. On 7th December 1857 the Ministers house was bought for £100. This cottage, which almost adjoins the chapel, was named 'The Manse' and was originally a teasel-growers cottage.

When Jane Crocker was baptised in 1860 it was recorded that 6 ladies had made 3 black gowns for ladies and one for the Pastor for Baptising. The material cost £1-14-0.

The Golden Jubilee of the foundation of the Baptist Church was held on Tuesday May 8th, 1866, when 220 sat down to Tea.

Isle Abbots and Fivehead were united under one Pastor, Mr John Burnham in 1874. In 1875 he appointed 2 Deacons at Isle Abbots, Mr. Tapp and H. Adams. In 1878 Mr. John Compston moved into Fivehead and led both Chapels. In December 1878 74 members signed a petition to Parliament "against the war upon Afghanistan".

When Miss Humphry of Woodlands retired as organist in 1874 she donated her Harmonium and left £100 to the Chapel. With this money the trustees bought a piece of land called "Wood". These 2 acres were later requisitioned by the Air Ministry for building Merryfield Airfield in 1942 and they paid £100 for them. After the war the land was offered back to the Chapel but they declined.

In August 1882 7 new trustees were appointed for Isle Abbots Chapel property, including one agricultural implement maker, 5 farmers and 1 farmer's son. The appointment had to be done again in December because it had not been written on stamped paper, nor signed at the meeting.

Isle Abbots had a close association with Fivehead Chapel where Benjamin Bicknell was baptised. After his marriage to the organist there, Rosie Wilcox, they moved to Bromes Farm in 1892 and continued to attend at Isle Abbots.

In 1895 under the pastorate of Rev. Edward S Hadler, both Fivehead and Isle Abbots Chapels joined the Christian Endeavour Society. Mr. Hadler reported to the Western Baptist Association in 1898 that "The C. E. Societies at Fivehead and Isle Abbots have proved helpful to the young people, who have sought to assist the needy, visit the sick and aged; they have likewise taken part in Evangelistic work …Open Air Services on the hills and at other places have proved attractive and a power for good; whilst Pastoral Visitation has led to some remarkable conversions of persons who did not attend any place of worship. So we thank God and take courage".

A wedding report in 1898 reads "A very pretty wedding took place at Isle Abbots on August 16th when Lilian Staple Mead, daughter of Rev. Silas Mead of London and formerly of South Australia was married to Mr. Crosbie C Brown of Harley St. College. Mr Mead had brought his daughter to the country where he had lived as a boy, that she might be married among his own people and amidst the beautiful scenery of the pleasant fields of Somerset. The wedding took place from Mrs. Uttermare's house, who was the brides aunt. Afterwards Mr & Mrs. Hallett of Swell Court received them. The ceremony was performed by Rev. G. A. James, B.A., minister of Fivehead and Isle Abbots Baptist Churches and Rev. Silas Mead." "The bride was almost dark enough for an Eastern Beauty". Silas Mead had been born in Isle Abbots and later became minister of the newly formed Baptist Church, Adelaide, South Australia.

People can remember Sunday School parties at the Chapel in the 1950s. A Postcard exists of a 'Sunday School Treat' in July 1905 at Bromes Farm. R.E. Bicknell sent it to someone in Taunton on 25/10/1905 saying "Many happy returns from all. This is a photo of our Sunday School taken when the treat was held here in July." The large number of children and adults look very splendid in their best clothes.

Sunday School treat at Bromes Farm, July 1905

In 1907 plans were made to celebrate the Centenary of Isle Abbots Baptist Church in the following year. Land for stables was bought for £4.10s.0d. Stables and trap house, furnace house and offices and a wall round the burial ground were all built for £87. The Chapel, Schoolrooms and classrooms were renovated for £30. A brass plate was placed in the vestibule to mark the grave of Rev. William Humphry. The total cost proved to be £150 and £120 had been promised when the great day arrived. The actual centenary was June 23rd when the Rev. Principal W. J. Henderson B.A. of Bristol preached at the afternoon service. The congregation then moved to Manor Farm for tea. The County Gazette, which gave a column and a half to its account, described the scene as "Quite the largest gathering seen in Isle Abbots for many years". There was an arch of evergreens and flowers in the barn, and in the next building tea had been prepared by the Ladies' Committee, with the help of the minister's wife, Mrs. Schofield. Nearly 250 folk sat down to tea.

In 1916 the children of Isle Abbots Sunday School gave the money for their prizes to a Prisoner of War fund known as "Somersets in Germany".

At the end of the First World War a united church meeting between Fivehead and Isle Abbots Baptists was held in Isle Abbots, preceded by tea and concluded with a Communion Service. This united service became an annual event held in each village alternately.

In 1935 there were 9 baptisms in Isle Abbots and the church membership stood at 41.

Jim Slade died in 1936; he had been a member of Isle Abbots Chapel for 43 years and for many years deacon, secretary and treasurer. The tribute to him in the Church Book speaks of him as "scrupulously fair, honoured for his integrity of character, kindly in nature and a true friend… One who wholly followed the Lord his God". His son Arthur succeeded him in his office. The church invited Mrs Jim Slade to become a deacon but she felt she could not accept the honour. Willie Clarke and Tom Derrick were elected deacons.

Electric lights were installed in the Chapel between 1942-1943.

When Miss Lane, who for many years had been the tenant of Isle Abbots Manse died the trustees recommended the church to sell the property. In 1951 it was sold at auction for £1,000 and the money invested.

In June 1952 the church received an unexpected gift of £10.10s.0d from Isle Abbots Cricket XI.

Rev C Plumb installed electric heating and an electric organ blower in 1963.

In 1966 the Rev. H. Nutkins left the Church at Hatch Beauchamp and became Pastor of Fivehead and Isle Abbots where he worked until he retired in 1974. The Revd. E. Hough, F.R.G.S. took over the pastorate of both Chapels in 1975 followed by Pastor Mike Jarrett in 1978.

The Revd. Berkley Johnson was called to the pastorate of both Chapels in 1979 and lived in the Manse at Fivehead. A dedicated and dearly loved Pastor, Mr. Johnson along with is wife Alice was also active in helping to run the Isle Abbots Friendship Club.

In 2002 a village history exhibition was mounted in the Church Room to mark the Golden Jubilee of the reign of Queen Elizabeth II. The pastor

Mrs Butler Preaching, Christmas 1999

at that time, Mrs Joyce Butler wrote the following:-

"In 1992 the two Churches agreed to call their own Ministers and Mrs Joyce Butler assumed the pastorate of Isle Abbots. During this period the Lord has led the fellowship forward in a remarkable way. A new roof has been added to the Chapel, the hall and rooms at the rear of the building have been renovated and modern kitchen and toilet facilities added. This work was mainly carried out by a dedicated group within the fellowship. The whole area now forms a small conference centre, which is not only used by our own Association but by other Christian denominations who seek peace and spiritual refreshment within a quiet country setting.

At the end of 1994 the same group decided to build a Baptistry and on Easter Day 1995 Alun Carp became the first candidate to be baptized."

~~~~~~~~~~

The Chapel interior showing the upstairs gallery

Sadly the congregation dwindled, mainly due to the older supporters in the village passing away and on 3rd December 2006 the last service was held before the chapel was sold and subsequently converted to a house. Part of the graveyard has been preserved and accessible, but other gravestones have been moved to make a garden.

Mrs Frances Burgess who had been organist and faithful worshipper at the Chapel for many years played at the final service. At one time Mr Bill Clarke kept the graveyard in immaculate condition and was often seen walking through the village carrying his gardening tools. Older residents can remember Sunday School Christmas parties and the annual outing to Weymouth by charabanc where they would play on the beach followed by tea at Browns Café. Members of the Parish Church would often join in special services such as Harvest and Carols.

Baptist Chapel cup and saucer

~~~ Farming ~~~
The Main Farms, their Occupants and Labourers

Isle Abbots was primarily a farming village until the advent of the motorcar, which allowed people to travel further afield to work. Most farms were mixed with dairy, sheep and arable. They would employ many more labourers than today, on a much smaller acreage. Indeed the milking of 14 cows at Bromes Farm was listed as a major asset when it was sold in 1918. Many of the farms were in the hands of landlords who rented out the farm and cottages for the labourers. The farm labourers wives would be at home looking after the house and children and often working at home making gloves, collars or shirts. Some would be employed as domestic help in the farmhouses or as dairywomen. It was still evident in the 1970s that some of the older farm workers wives still cleaned at the bigger houses.

Dick Lucas and John Humphry discussing field names after dinner at Lower Woodlands

Some of the interesting old field names probably date back to medieval times when land was cultivated on a communal basis and the majority of people could not read or write. The words orchard, meadow, copse or field would be prefixed by something descriptive such as higher, lower, home or mill and thus describing the location, the type of crop grown there or the owner. These names still exist today but have sometimes become corrupted and of course many small fields have been incorporated into bigger fields.

A major crop in this area was teasels. The cultivation of teasels to be used in the finishing processes of woollen cloth was in practice by Tudor times. Although modern machines using wire brushes were introduced, teasels were preferred for certain cloth right up until the 1960s. The teasels were picked by hand and gathered into groups called 'hands' and then tied on long poles about 7ft high and left to dry upright in the field or in a barn spread on sheets to catch the seeds. They would then be sewn into sacks and sent by train from Hatch Beauchamp to the woollen mills, mainly in Yorkshire. Teasels now grow wild around the field edges, particularly near the Fivehead River.

Cider apple orchards were also very important. Labourers were often supplied with cider whilst at work and this was considered as part of their wages. The apples would be allowed to fall to the ground when ripe and then collected by hand and put in sacks. The sacks would be transported to the farm where many farmers made their own cider or sent to cider presses like Perry's at Dowlish Wake. This continued to a smaller degree until the 1990s when the harvesting of the fruit from old trees became uneconomical.

With the introduction of the tractor and other machines farms became bigger and under private ownership, used far fewer employees.

Polly and Tom Derrick picking teasels c.1920

Loading Teasels c.1920. Edward Barrington, Son Edward and labourer

Collecting apples at Cuffs Orchard - date unknown

MANOR FARM

This farm was originally known as Whitebarne Pound and farmed by Richard Lamprey and his sons John and Henry. They had requested permission from the Earl of Hertford for a dwelling on a small piece of land known by this name.

By 1841 the land was being farmed by John and Zebulon Page. They were looked after by a housekeeper, Mary Stacey and a 14-year-old servant, Lucy Winnil. It was shown as having 150 acres employing 5 men and 2 boys. By 1871 the acreage had risen to 286 and farmed by Jennings and Fanny Still.

In 1873 *The Imperial Gazetteer of England and Wales* records that the manor of Isle Abbots belongs to the Duchy of Cornwall. And thus began the Duchy ownership of the farm now known as Manor Farm. It is recorded that in 1881 John and Mary Palmer and their 3 children and a servant lived there employing 8 men and 3 boys.

This Duchy-owned farm has now been in the Humphry family for four generations, beginning with John and Gertrude about 1888. Son John (known as Jack) and wife Annie then took over. Jack had been born at Woodlands Farm, Isle Abbots and Annie (nee Glide) at Manor Farm Curry Mallet.

Jack was a member of the Baptist Chapel and Annie Church of England. Until the age of 16 their son Richard attended Church one week and Chapel the other. Then he was allowed to decide for himself and chose to belong to the Church.

When Richard was County Chairman for Young Farmers he met Doreen who was County Executive and when they became engaged, Jack and Annie built the bungalow known as Greystones and moved into it in 1957 just before Doreen and Richard were married. Doreen's father advised her that if she wanted anything major altered in the house it was best to get it done in the first six months of marriage whilst her husband was still keen to please! She remembered this and had the old backhouse knocked down. The backhouse was no longer used for anything, although at one time all the cooking and washing would have been done there and possibly some farm hands would have slept upstairs. The kitchen window looked straight out onto the grey

Mark and Belinda Humphry with children Matthew and Hannah outside Manor Farm, 2002

stone walls and Doreen wanted to expose the view. Her mother-in-law said 'why didn't I do that years ago?'

There were two wells for the house. Only one tap just by the kitchen door supplied safe drinking water. All the other water for the house and farm was pumped from the river. When they went to bed they took a carafe of fresh water upstairs for drinking and teeth cleaning. There are two big water tanks at the end of the house and the water is still pumped by ram pumps all the way across the fields from the river by the weir. The purest water was reputed as coming from the well at Pitts Cottage. One of the wells is in the little orchard opposite Manor Farm.

When Doreen and Richard were first married, his mother Annie had 12 hours of domestic help in the house. Six hours from Mrs Manning and six from Lily Mear. Annie kept on Mrs Manning at her new bungalow and Lily Mear stayed at the farm. The milkers all wore white overalls and it was Doreen's job to wash these. She kept an eye on the animals at lambing and calving time and was often sent off to various places to fetch spares for machinery and to do the banking and collect wages from Ilminster. Payday used to be on Monday every other week. Workers were also given two rows of potatoes, free milk and cider.

Richard and Doreen had four children, Jennifer, Mark, Andrew and Alison. When Jennifer their first child was born, Lily Mear knitted beautiful clothes for the baby and Doreen remembers all the farm staff being excited at the arrival as they felt part of the family.

The Queen and Prince Phillip made an official visit to Manor Farm in 1966. Prince Charles still visits occasionally but his visits are not made known to the general public.

Richard was Churchwarden for many years and later Church Treasurer. He was also Chairman of the Parish Council. He died suddenly in 1993. He was always a kind and helpful person and one of life's gentlemen.

When Mark married Belinda they moved into Southey Farm, the milking unit across the river, just in Isle Brewers parish. There had once been two brick built labourers cottages adjacent to Southey but these were demolished in the 1980s. Pitts cottages would also have housed workers for Manor Farm.

After Richard died Mark took over the running of the farm and the family, which now included Mathew and Hannah moved into the farmhouse. They gave up keeping sheep. The other members of the family had all moved away and Doreen moved to Broadway.

Mr. T. Channing who was a builder at Hatch Beauchamp left a helpful ledger of work carried out in Isle Abbots. It included work at Manor and Southay (Southey) Farms both belonging to the Duchy.

- 1891 repairing tiles and plaster on Southay cottages. 200 dark roman tiles. Carpenters labour 1/9d, mason & apprentice 7 days each £11.8.6d
- 1893 for Mr John Humphry repairing flood hatches on Manor Farm approx 6 days, 4 men from 7 to 13/- a day. Materials 6 tons building stone, lime, 1 load of coal ashes, cement, plus a contract for Southays cottages. Total £12.
- 1894 Manor of Ile Abbots Duchy of Cornwall at dwelling house & Pitts cottages, Southay Dairyhouse. Mason's labour 5/-, 25 tiles, 2 slates, 1 bucket of cement – total 14/-.

HRH Queen Elizabeth & Prince Philip talk to Richard and Doreen Humphry at Manor Farm. Daughter Jennifer behind.

TWO BRIDGES FARM

Two Bridges Farmhouse, 2002

The earliest census of 1841 records the prolific Winter family of John and Betsy with 8 children. Maybe the children were helpful harvesting the teasels that grew in that area. They were certainly there 20 years later but with only 3 adult children, 2 grandchildren, one lodger and a 12-year-old servant William Bowey.

By the 1880s Heman and Sara Patten were farming 110 acres with 2 women and 4 labourers and by the beginning of the next century John and Sarah Dare with 4 children were in residence and the family continued to farm there until the 1960s.

Two Bridges was originally part of the Coombs/Earnshill Estate but was sold to the local Council in 1919 under a scheme to set up small farms to provide work for men returning from the war.

George and Avril Withers moved into Two Bridges in 1966 after Mr and Mrs Dare had retired to Ilton. Along with their 4 children they quickly became part of the community. Their two eldest sons moved away and daughter Julie sadly had a brain tumour and was in a wheelchair for many years before she died. Their son Roger who was born with Special Needs loved to follow his father around the farm and was a very likeable young man.

The milking parlour was next to the road and George, who was always cheerful, could be heard singing or whistling whilst he milked the cows. George became well known for singing folk songs and was invited to sing around the country and even made some recordings. At village gatherings he re-wrote the words of traditional songs to bring in local names and events and his sister Marjorie would often accompany him on the piano. George also helped organise children (and often reluctant adults) to take part in singing and acting.

One song referring to the Chestnut Tree planted in the middle of the road at Cox's Pit for the Queen Elizabeth's Silver Jubilee was sung to the tune of The Red Flag.

> O Chestnut Tree
> O Chestnut Tree
> Our visual amenity
> The trouble with our Chestnut Tree
> He's where he hadn't ought to be.
> Now, if we'd asked the R.D.C.
> In proper meek humility
> And begged for their authority
> We'd get it by next Jubilee.

When the road outside Two Bridges became flooded George often ferried children from the school bus through the water and helped rescue marooned cars. They only ever had water in the house once in July 1968 when they had a visitor and had settled down to watch wrestling on the television. They were eating cheese and cream crackers and Avril was shelling peas when they heard a strange noise outside. They opened the front door to find the floods had come up in a couple of hours and the water rushed in. The dog was around the back and was let in through the window and scattered the peas and tin of biscuits off the table and they were all floating in the water. Avril's bantams were drowned but nothing else lost.

Roger, Avril and George Withers at their leaving party
Mrs Massman and Mrs Priddle behind

In 1988 they took a small council holding in Horton for a while before retiring to a bungalow in Horton naming it Stemalong after the road in Isle Abbots and Roger went to live in sheltered accommodation. They continued to join in village events regularly and George sang in the choir and provided entertainment at Village Hall events until they were no longer able. They have both now passed away.

The Farm was then rented to Mr and Mrs Andrew Farley who lived there for a few years with their two daughters. It was then sold to Mr and Mrs Richard Westworth. Some of the old barns have now been converted into a house for their son Timothy and family.

George Withers wrote a beautiful poem, which referred to his earlier married life when they were renting a holding. Although it does not refer to Isle Abbots it is a fitting memorial to a couple who were very much part of the village for some years.

MILKING ON THE MOOR

We were young, we were poor when we milked on the moor, and our assets were pitifully small.
Ten cows and a horse were our only resource, a cow dog and that's about all.
We kept old fashioned Devons and a Shorthorn or two and old Kit in the shaft of the float.
A couple of buckets and stools that was all of our tools, except this cap and me brown smock coat.

We took two or three churns down to bring home the milk and a strainer for cow hairs and flies.
A twice a day chore milking down on the moor, with Sundays and weekdays the same.
But we said we could do it and buckled down to it. Well farming's that kind of a game.

When the sharp bubbling sound of a Curlew floats down, it's a call that goes straight to my heart.
And the smooth emerald green of the weed on the reen, where the dragonflies hover and dart,
the hum of the bees, the pail 'tween my knees and the horse half asleep by the gate on the point of one shoe,
you know how they do in a comotosed sort of a state.

Yes, was lovely down there with the rooks in the air and the sweet smell of Cowslips and May.
And a fresh trodden grass like a dream from the past.
God I wish I could smell it today.

'Twas a life without frills, but it just paid the bills for the nippers and me and the wife.
Paid for meat on the table, a ton of Red Label, the rent, the essentials of life.

But those days are gone and the world has moved on to things that are much less ethereal.
To quotas and clothes, keeping up with the Jones and emails and such things material.
But if I could change tracks I would turn my old back on this 21st Century allure.
To the prime of my life, when I took my young wife and old Kit milking down on the moors.

WOODLANDS, HIGHER WOODLANDS and LOWER WOODLANDS

There were a lot of changes around the Woodlands area over the years. The acreage of each farm depending on the frequent changes in ownership of individual fields. Also the various cottages occupied by workers at the different farms make the history difficult to untangle. Some farm labourers' cottages have merged into bigger houses and some have gone altogether. Old barns from these farms have been converted making new homes.

LOWER WOODLANDS

This farmhouse was built around 1600. Sometimes referred to as School Farm as it was in trust to Langport Grammar School. It was being farmed by various members of the Baker family certainly from 1841 when the farmer was Robert.

In 1851 it was listed as having 190 acres. By 1861 the farmer was a younger Robert with 3 children and 15-year-old dairymaid, Emily. But by 1871 there appeared to be only 67 acres employing one man and one boy farmed by William Abbott. However by 1881 it was back to 150 acres with 6 labourers and Charles Stuckey as the farmer. By 1891 the head was listed as William Adams, dairyman.

From the beginning of the 20th century we see Job Crocker as the farmer, listed as a Shepherd. The Crocker family lived in cottages around the Roundoak area for some time, with Job himself being a ploughboy at the age of 10.

After Job Crocker came another Job, this time Job Trott with his wife Lillian and daughter Mabel. When Mabel married Mr Downton and had 2 daughters, the house, which fortunately had two staircases, was roughly divided for the two families but there was only one downstairs bathroom, which was accessed from either side. Job died from injuries received when he fell into a bonfire at the house. The property, together with outbuildings and 57 acres was sold to Dick Lucas of Higher Woodlands in 1975. The house and a small piece of land was then divided off and sold to his daughter Susan and her husband Mervyn Vickery in October that year and they are still there today. Susan and Mervyn had a lot of work to do on the house as well as raising 5 children there. Susan started the Isle Abbots Playgroup and the whole family have taken part in village activities over the years.

WOODLANDS

The earliest part of this farmhouse is 16th Century with an extension built in 1736. It is believed that the Poorhouse was once here.

The farm has been in the Humphry family for many years. In 1841 Edward Humphry aged 30 lived there with wife Eliza and by 1851 Edward was shown as farming 250 acres employing 11 labourers. By 1861 the couple had 5 children Susan, Eliza, Mary, Edward and John and a Governess and two servants living there.

The family name continued and the last census in 1911 showed Edward age 55 and son Henry 21, which is when we come into living memory, as Henry, known as Harry, became father to John the present owner-occupier.

John was born at the farm in 1922 attended by the district nurse. His mother was Edith Rose Richards from North Curry. John and his brother Edward went to the village school and then on to Ilminster Grammar School.

When John was young they kept Turkeys that were sold to a butcher in Ilminster. The dairy unit was at Broadfields with 35 cows and they kept 6 cows at the farmhouse milked by Jack Shepherd. The thatched property at Broadfields was sold in 1972 to pay towards Edward's share of the farm after their parents' death.

John remembers his father being the first in the village to own a car.

James (Jim) Mead was the carter at Woodlands and his wife Ivy was a servant girl. During the war 100

Lower Woodlands 1975

Lower Woodlands, 2002
Sue and Mervyn Vickery with William, Martha, Emma and grandaughter Rosalie

Harry, Edith and John Humphry

Aerial view of Broadfields Farm

acres of their farm was compulsorily purchased to make the airfield and some of the labourers' cottages and a smallholding disappeared. John vaguely remembers Miss Lane and Drakes shop and when Mr Drake delivered the mail before Polly Adams took over, and Jack Adams driving their milk lorry.

Harry Humphry with turkeys

John met Nancy on a coach outing from Ilton to a Pantomime in Bath. They married in 1957. Nancy came from a farming family just down the road at Ilford. They had two daughters Carol and Susan who both married but stayed in the area.

Because they were on the edge of the village John can't remember being very involved in village activities when he was younger. But they joined in things more after he retired and at one time Nancy ran the Whist Club in the church room.

A barn near the farmhouse has been converted into a private house called **WOODLANDS BARN** and the majority of the land is currently let out to neighbouring farmers.

Harry driving hay cart, Jack Adams on top

Jack Adams driving tractor with Harry behind

HIGHER WOODLANDS

Aerial view of Higher Woodlands, 1964

Higher Woodlands Barn 2002
John & Diane Lucas with Thomas, Adam, David, Toby and Oliver

Higher Woodlands Farm, once owned by the Earl of Egremont, has seen many different owners and tenant farmers. The farm as we know it today consists of land acquired from other farms and smallholdings over the years. Dick (Richard) Lucas is retired and son John now runs the farm along with four of his sons.

Dick was born in 1919 to a farming family in Puckington and his wife Rosalie came from Fort William. They bought **ASHFORD FARM** with 100 acres and built a new house there in 1952. They then bought Higher Woodlands in 1959 and the farmhouse there remained occupied for some time by the cowman Mr Reeves and his many children.

Dick and Rosalie brought up their 4 daughters and one son at the Ashford house and only moved to the Woodlands Farmhouse when son John married Diane so that they could live at Ashford. After Rosalie died and John was running the farm he converted **BARNS AT HIGHER WOODLANDS** to accommodate their growing family of 5 sons and sold the Ashford house. Later came another barn conversion for son Thomas and family.

Mr Webber, a cowman, lived in a house known as **ASHFORD COTTAGE** for about 20 years but this was sold and two other nearby barns converted to houses. One was bought by Dick's daughter Sara and her husband & named **THE OLD TRACTOR HOUSE** and the other was called **ASHFORD BARN**.

After living alone for many years Dick

Dick Lucas showing the champion of the Christmas Fatstock Show in Ilminster, c.1961
(from the Chard & Ilminster News)

married again but his wife Mary died in 2000 after only a few years together. Dick is now in his 90s and still living in the farmhouse and has many grandchildren and great grandchildren.

Land at Broadfields was added to the Higher Woodlands estate and a new cowman's' house built along with a dairy unit. The original old thatched Broadfields farmhouse (often referred to as Broadlands) having been knocked down in the 1970s. They also bought Bromes Farm and its modern bungalow and buildings where John and Diane's son Daniel keeps goats. Their sons Tom and Toby work on the farm and Adam lives and farms a suckler herd just in the Fivehead parish. Youngest son Oliver is currently studying music at university.

ASHFORD OLD FARMHOUSE

Just on the edge of the village boundary to the South, this 16th Century thatched farmhouse has been in private ownership for many years and not attached to any of its original land. One notable occupant was John Pytt (Pitt). The house has changed hands many times.

Ashford Old Farmhouse

NORTHALLS FARM

The earliest part of this thatched farmhouse was built in the 16th century. The farm had been part of the Pyne Estate for many years and was up for sale by the R. T. Combes Trust in 1930 by which time Mr Edward Barrington had been in occupation for over 50 years. In 1841 it was farmed by William Tilley, with his wife Frances and 6 children. By 1851 Frances was a widow and son Thomas the farmer, employing 6 labourers. Richard Whittle followed and then came the Barringtons. Mr Edgar Habberfield purchased the farm and the sale included the farmhouse next door known as Marshes (originally Stills Farmhouse) and Uttermares cottages next to the church. Conditions of the sale provided that Mr and Mrs Barrington could stay living in Northalls and Mr and Mrs Habberfield would live at Marshes but have access to all the farm and outbuildings with the exception of the Back Kitchen.

The sales brochure described Marshes as a "pretty old fashioned residence with a good garden and a stone built range of buildings consisting of stalls for 8 cows, stabling for 3 horses, a loose box, barn, granary, coal house, garage and wagon shed." Marshes was originally known as **STILLS FARMHOUSE**. In 1841 Elizabeth Still was 87 living with 3 sons and by 1851 Jennings Still was farming 47 acres employing 1 man. The 1901 census shows it as being 2 cottages, Marshes 1 & 2. It was later called Saddlers, then renamed Horsefeathers but has now reverted back to its original name of Stills Farmhouse. So this 'pretty old fashioned residence' has seen many changes. The barns were sold and converted to a house known as **SADDLERS BARN.**

Mr and Mrs Edward Barrington (nee Humphry)

Cows were milked at both Northalls and Marshes barn. Marshes was the first to have electricity so an electric milking machine was installed there. Don

A young Bernard Habberfield in the garden of Marshes

Tapp hand milked the cows at Northalls and Edgar would bring the milk 2 buckets at a time on a yoke down to Marshes to put through the cooler. Then the milk would be collected together in churns and put on the barn ledge right by the road where there is now a big window at the front of Saddlers Barn.

Buildings before conversion to Sadlers Barn

Edgar and Bessie Habberfield brought up their 6 children at Marshes before moving into Northalls farmhouse. Violet the eldest was 17 when they moved into Isle Abbots and was expected to stay at home to help her mother around the house. She married Harry Priddle and stayed in the village. Then there was Sylvia, Marjorie, Mary, Leslie and Bernard. The younger children went to the village school. Bernard and Leslie stayed at home and worked on the farm. Sadly Leslie died aged only 28 from a disease contracted from the poultry that he reared. Marshes farmhouse was sold and Bernard and his wife Dulcie, who came from Barrington, built a new bungalow next to Stills barns, which they then called Marshes. This is where they lived with their children Anthony and Wendy until moving into Northalls when Edgar and Bessie died.

Edgar Habberfield at Northalls Farmhouse

The 1930 sale included 145 acres of land consisting of 30 different plots described as 'being in a very high state of cultivation' with charming names given to plots like 'Great Islemoor', 'Well Close' and 'Come by Chance' to name but a few. The farm has added extra land since.

At the same 1930 sale the Pyne Estate was selling 11 other lots of land and orchards in the village separately. Two cottages known as Cuffs and occupied by Mrs. Adams and Mr. Swayne each with 2 rooms downstairs and 2 rooms upstairs, along with an orchard. Other thatched cottages sold were in the occupation of Mr Hooper, and there was also a cottage, garden and enclosure of pastureland in the occupation of Mrs Taylor which was known as Lumbards.

Bernard Habberfield on Cider Press

Anthony and Wendy Habberfield remember their grandmother Bessie still using the Back House for all the cooking on a big oil cooker and the food would be carried across the yard to the house. There was a stone cobbled path between the house and the Back House among the muddy farmyard that Grandma used to scrub. It was covered over when the whole yard was concreted in the 1970s. Washday was Monday and water was heated in the Back

Aerial view of Sadlers Barns showing Stills Farmhouse, Marshes Bungalow, Two Steps and Waldrons Barns

Haywain at Northalls
Leslie Hooper, Edgar Habberfield, Don Tapp and others.
Bernard on horse, led by Bill Burton

House furnace. A tin bath was used on Sundays. When Commander Williams made an archaeological survey of the house in 1975 he described the building as having "an upstairs room reached by external stairs with replacement roof circa 1800. The ground floor had a large fireplace with oven lined with early bricks and fitted with an iron door and built within an earlier bacon chamber. In front of the oven is a furnace. The only concession to modernity is a low open sided grate on the hearth under which was a shallow oven, a type that appears to have been introduced 80-100 years ago".

Thatching straw in Townfield c.1965
Edgar, Anthony, Wendy and Bernard Habberfield

Anthony can remember when he broke his leg as a child. Don Tapp used to take him on the horse and cart to haul Mangolds from the field 'cum by chance'. He fell between the horse and the shafts. At one time the farm had a T20 tractor and a 3 ton trailer which was loaded by hand with Sugar Beet and taken to Hatch Beauchamp station where the Beet was chucked directly into a railway wagon ready to be collected.

Dulcie and Bernard made improvements to the farmhouse including a proper kitchen. In later years, between milking and working outdoors on the farm, Bernard and Tony spent many happy hours entertaining visitors in front of the Back House fireplace. Both Anthony and Wendy attended the village school until it closed in 1959 and they finished their education outside the village. Anthony moved into the Marshes bungalow when he married. Wendy and her son Alistair Richards later returned to the farmhouse to live.

Bernard Habberfield and grandson Alistair binding straw, early 1980's

Bernard and Anthony farmed together with the help of their cowman as they had a milking herd of Friesian cows as well as growing crops. Then they opted out of milking under a government incentive along with many other farmers who were encouraged to do so.

Another change came after Bernard died in 1999. Anthony continued to farm on his own with help and support from his second wife Mary. Dulcie, Wendy

Northalls Farmhouse - 2015

and son Alistair moved back to Marshes. After Dulcie died, Wendy and Alistair went to live in the two cottages at Uttermares; Northalls farmhouse was sold and renamed **CHAPEL FARMHOUSE** and the bungalow called Marshes also sold. Two barns were converted to private houses now known as **THE OLD COACH HOUSE** and **THE STABLES** and what was the Back House became a very nice house for Anthony and Mary, which they called Northalls Farm. New farm buildings were erected for housing cattle and storing grain and with a little outside help continues to be run as before.

Bernard was once churchwarden, followed later by Anthony who has had several spells in office. They have both served on the Parish Council and Anthony has been chairman since 1997. The farm has hosted many church fund raising events with the dedicated work of both Anthony and Mary Habberfield.

Northalls memories……… During a conversation with elderly sisters Betty and Joan Hurford at their house in North Curry in 1996, they told me some memories of Isle Abbots. (Ed.) Their mother was Mary Barrington who was born at Northalls in 1881 and lived there until 1912 with brother Edward and sisters Eliza and Sarah Jane and parents Edward and Susan. They remembered a housekeeper called Miss Hart and there was always a live in maid and Mary Adams did the washing 3 or 4 days a week. Their mother had a live in governess and the schoolroom was at the Ilminster end of Northalls.

The farm grew grain, kept sheep, cattle and pigs. Their grandfather Edward Barrington used to buy a truckload of coal and sell it to his workers. He kept 6d a week from their wages for shoes, which were bought from Dicks in Taunton. Grandfather would not have a wireless in the house in case it burnt the house down so they had to go to the Back House to listen. They remembered him as always sitting by the fire.

BROMES HOUSE AND FARM

The earliest part of this house is thought to have been built around 1570. A stone above the central porch bears the date of 1627. Members of the Bromes family lived in the house for over 200 years. Within the house are jointed crucks and some rare plaster decorations, the odd bearded heads bearing a resemblance to the popular Green Man Motif.

Apart from farming, some members of the Bromes family appeared to be quite wealthy, or married into wealthy families. However, in 1687 reference is made by the Commissioners of the Treasury of the petition received from Mary Collins, widow, for a grant to her daughter Jane Brome of an estate of £18 per annum in Horton, forfeited by her husband John Brome who was in the rebellion and condemned to die. His brother was also in the rebellion but absconded till the general pardon. "The petitioner and her daughter who has 4 children and no maintenance having much suffered for being Kings evidence". John Brome was sentenced to be hanged at Glastonbury, but died before this could take place.

Phillip Brome was married to Martha, daughter of Sir John Knight of Bristol in 1648. The Knights were in the sugar business and three of their sons Phillip, Francis and Laurence Brome became members of the Society of Merchant Venturers. Young Phillip left to run a plantation on the Island of Nevis in the West Indies where he married Christiana Chapman. Phillip died on Nevis aged 52 and his tombstone is inscribed with a lengthy eulogy describing him as a man devoted to King and Church, renowned in the African trade, or less politely, slave trading. He settled £3,000 on his wife Christiana, his (silver) plate was in the care of his mother-in-law Mrs Mary Helme of London, his father Phillip and mother Martha of Ile Abbots were also legatees.

In 2012 Barbara Rickitt of Bromes House visited Nevis and located the graves of Phillip and Christiana Brome in the churchyard of St.Thomas Lowland. The gravestones are now somewhat broken but still legible.

An inventory of goods of Phillip Brome of Isle Abbots on 2nd October 1791 reads: –

'Hay, a small quantity of peas, one chest of drawers and one bed which were taken for the Lord's heriot' – (a late example of feudal dues). Several beds and

In 1842 John Scott Gould owned Bromes Farm when it was let to Samuel Humphry. By 1861 his widow Emma Humphry was the farmer with 117 acres employing 5 men and 2 boys. Major Barratt then purchased the farm.

By 1871 William Goodland was the farmer with his wife Susanna and sons John and Benjamin. Succeeded by son Benjamin and wife Jemima who lived in the farmhouse with their servant Rosa Aldridge aged 18.

Mr Channing a builder sent a bill to Major Barratt in 1892 for digging a new well at Mr Ben Bicknells (Bromes Farm). It was 23ft 6ins deep. The first 10 feet were charged at 2/- per ft, second 10 feet at 2/6 and the last 3ft 6in at 3/-. The stoning up at 1/- per foot, 7/- for driving away the clay, 3/- for digging a well drain, 53 foot of new lead at 1/6 a foot, 9 tons building stone and 2 tons of rough paviour were also supplied. Mr Channing also made a note in his ledger in 1909 that another well in Mr Bicknell's rickyard had 4ft 4ins of water and was 31ft deep.

Benjamin and Rosina Bicknell moved to Bromes Farm after farming in Fivehead. They had five children, Katherine (kit), Minnie, Benjamin, Thomas,

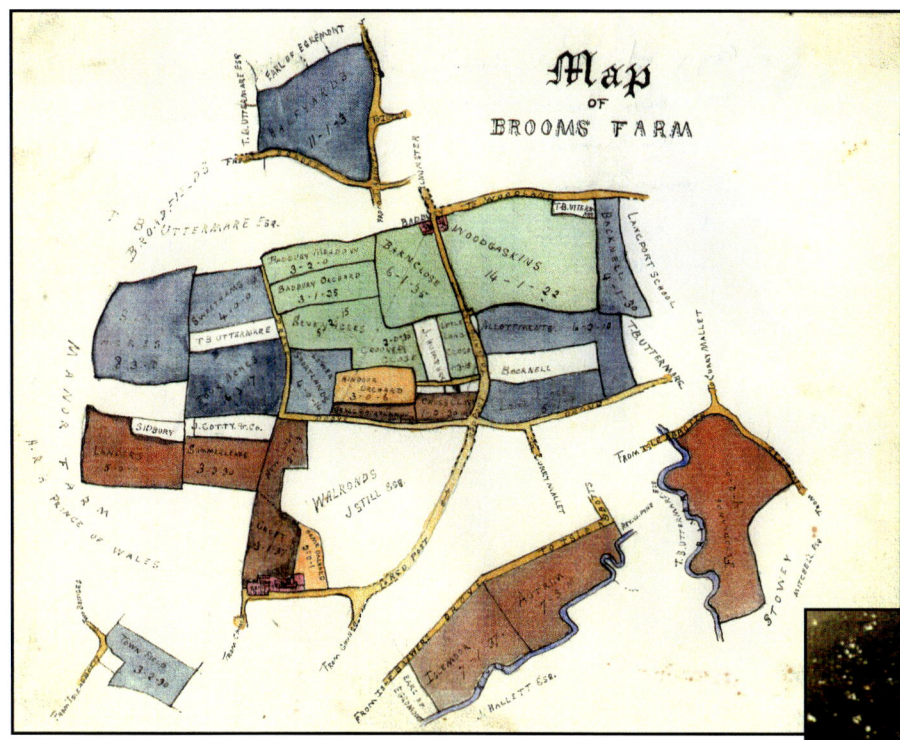

Hand drawn map of Bromes Farm found in an exercise book of a member of the Goodland family, drawn probably about 1900. Rather confusingly, North is at the foot of the map.

chairs, items such as a saddle, bridle and pillion, a cheese press, pewter dishes and books; 2 spitts, 1 dripping tray, 2 racks, 2 firedogs, a crane, a crook and a jack.

There are tabletop tombs in the churchyard and memorials on the floor in the chancel to various members of the Bromes family who were obviously quite prominent in the area. The first entry of a Brome in the church registers was in 1586 when Robert son of Christopher was baptised and the last entry in 1814 when William Brome married Sarah Yard also of Isle Abbots. It would appear that some of the female Bromes stayed in the village marrying into the Humphry and Cuff families.

The farm then passed to landholders and let out to local farmers.

Benjamin Bicknell and family c.1910

John and William. A servant Margaret Edmonds assisted the family. When Margaret married William Swain in the Baptist Chapel the Bicknells paid for the wedding.

The Bicknell's 21-year-old son John was killed in 1917 and is buried in Ypres Reservoir cemetery. Benjamin died after his motorbike collided with George Sealey's pony cart along Stemalong. It was dark and neither vehicle had lights. The shaft of the cart struck his chest and he was carried back to Bromes on a gate and a doctor called. It was believed that cracked ribs had punctured his lungs. At the time of the accident Benjamin was going to Fivehead for the thatcher to come to thatch the rick that Albert Adams had been building.

A special occasion -when B Bicknell provided a sack for the race

The farm was sold in 1918 so it is likely that is the point when Benjamin Bicknell purchased it before dying in 1925. The sales brochure describes it as a 'Small Freehold Estate for Dairy, Sheep and Corn' with 151 acres. The Farm Residence with 6 bedrooms, the kitchen having a Hearth Oven, Baking Oven and Ironing Stove and the Back Kitchen with 2 Furnaces, Pump, Well and Trough. Adjoining the house was a cider cellar. Outside were various barns, cattle Linhay, (open-fronted cattle sheds), Wagon House, stables, piggeries etc.

MARCH 31, 1921. THE CHRIST

Old Couple Congratulated by the King.—Mr. and Mrs. Frederick Wilcox, of Ile Abbots, Taunton, celebrated recently their diamond wedding anniversary, they having been married in 1861 at the Baptist Church, Cullompton. Mr. Wilcox is now 92, and his wife 82, years old. Both are in excellent health, and Mr. Wilcox is still able to read without glasses. Up

MR. AND MRS. FREDERICK WILCOX.
(Topical Press Agency.)

to eleven years ago he was engaged in farming, having successfully farmed on his own account for upwards of sixty years. The old people spent a happy day at the home of one of their sons, where a large family party assembled to celebrate the anniversary. They were surrounded by their ten children, twenty-three grandchildren, and two great-grandchildren. They received a letter of congratulation from the King, an honour they greatly esteemed.

At Badbury there was the Dairy House and across the road the Barton with cow stalls for 14 cows, calving pens, piggeries etc. A detached cottage now known as Little Flitters occupied by Harry Adams, and nearby two cottage tenements known as "Humphrey's Cottages" with an orchard. One occupied by Thomas Adams and the other by Simeon Mear.

The brochure elaborates with "The Estate is a very attractive Holding. It has kindly, healthy and productive soil, the Arables being congenial for root and corn crops, the Meadows and Pastures are sweet feeding and embrace some first class dairy land supplied with good water and the orchards are well stocked with good Cider and other fruit. The Chard Dairy Factory motor lorry calls at Badbury each day, thus affording an easy and inexpensive market for the milk."

The Farm continued in the hands of Bicknells until Billy (William) and his wife Renee retired. As they didn't have any children the farm was then sold in 1962 and they built a house named Cross Close on the site of two old labourers cottages for themselves.

BROMES MEMORIES ……… In 1992 when an elderly Ethel Patterson (nee Wilcox) came to the village to visit graves in the Chapel yard, she visited Bromes House and had a look around. She later wrote her thanks saying "Isle Abbots has such a special place in my heart. I spent all my holidays since I was four with my Grandmother Wilcox and her family at Badbury. (Ethel's aunt was Mrs Bicknell at Bromes Farm. It reminded me of the lovely times we all had during Christmas when the younger cousins went outside to sing carols. What memories!" Ethel remembers Bill and Renee having a housekeeper Miss Follett and Maggie Swain who was a general worker in the house and on the farm.

Bromes Farmhouse, 1960's

Aerial view of Bromes Farm 1973

Richard had his own Jersey calf for Christmas when he was only 8 years old and Buttercup later became the centre of the holding with her rich milk rearing calves and used for cheese, cream, yoghurt, butter and ice cream. Piglets were raised on the whey and a variety of sheep, chickens, bantams and ducks joined

The next owners were the Saynor family. The farm by then had 77 acres with the barns at Badbury but had lost the Dairy House. Then in 1973 it was sold again to Mr John Down from Dowlish Wake who divided off the old farmhouse together with 6 acres from the farm. Mr Down continued to run the farm and built some new buildings and a manager's bungalow opposite Little Flitters, which he then sold. The old barns and piggeries at Badbury were also sold for conversion to a house known as Badbury Barton.

The farmhouse, which henceforth was known as Bromes House, was then sold on quickly to Patrick and Sarah Scott who modernised it and joined the cider barn to the main house where they lived with their 4 children.

In 1979 the property changed hands again when Martin and Barbara Rickitt and children Richard and Rachel moved in. Whilst Martin was still running his business in London, Barbara developed a smallholding on the 6 acres.

Anthony Habberfield making hay for the smallholding at Bromes House 1993

- 57 -

the family. Two areas of woodlands were planted and the old ponds dug out. Together with the vegetable patch this holding continued to provide good food for the family until the children left home and the animals were phased out. The productive grass fields now provide good hay for a neighbouring farm and a home for the Isle Abbots Railway, which has been developed since 2001. This 7¼in gauge line now extends to over half a mile and gives pleasure to visitors as well as raising funds for village causes on event days.

Thatching the North side of Bromes House c.2000

Mr Downs sold the rest of the farm with its modern well-equipped dairy unit and 104 acres to Mr Speakman. He was not there for long before he sold it to Mr D Gaydon. In 1995 the farm was up for sale again and purchased by John Lucas from Higher Woodlands. With the dairy unit for Higher Woodlands being at Broadfields the milking unit at Bromes was converted for milking goats by Daniel Lucas and the bungalow is lived in by Daniel and his family. The rest of the land is farmed jointly with Higher Woodlands Farm.

WELLINGS FARM

Also known as Wellinge, Wellinch, Willing Farm. On the borders of the parish of Curry Mallet, this farm is worth a mention. Records show that Isle Abbots were responsible for building an access bridge over the Fivehead River, but that Wellinge Farm should repair it. However, a charge on the parish rate book shows an entry for hewing and hauling wood for repairs. The bridge was built in 1751 and the stone piers still remain. This farm was only accessible on foot from Isle Abbots, taking Ball Lane to the bridge where the baker and postman would leave their wares. Another footpath led to Curry Mallet. Although remains were still visible in the 1970's, the house and buildings are now totally eradicated.

Anthony Habberfield can remember visiting the farm as a young boy when an old lady called Mrs Dyte lived there and kept lots of goats. When she was taken off to hospital there was good furniture inside and a pianola, but the house and farm buildings were left to fall into disrepair and cattle went inside and it was eventually bulldozed. At one time members of the Taylor family lived in the farmhouse. The Taylors had previously lived at Lombards.

Audrey, Phyl and Betty Winter with their Granny Caroline (Taylor) at Wellings Farm, 1935

Betty Sheale recalls how she and her sisters Audrey and Phyl spent many happy summer holidays with her Gran Caroline Taylor at Wellinge Farm.

Isle Abbots Farmers c.1920's - unknown location
Harry Tapp, Mr. Glide, Jack Humphry, Harry Humphry, Wilfred & Alan Garland, Edward Barrington

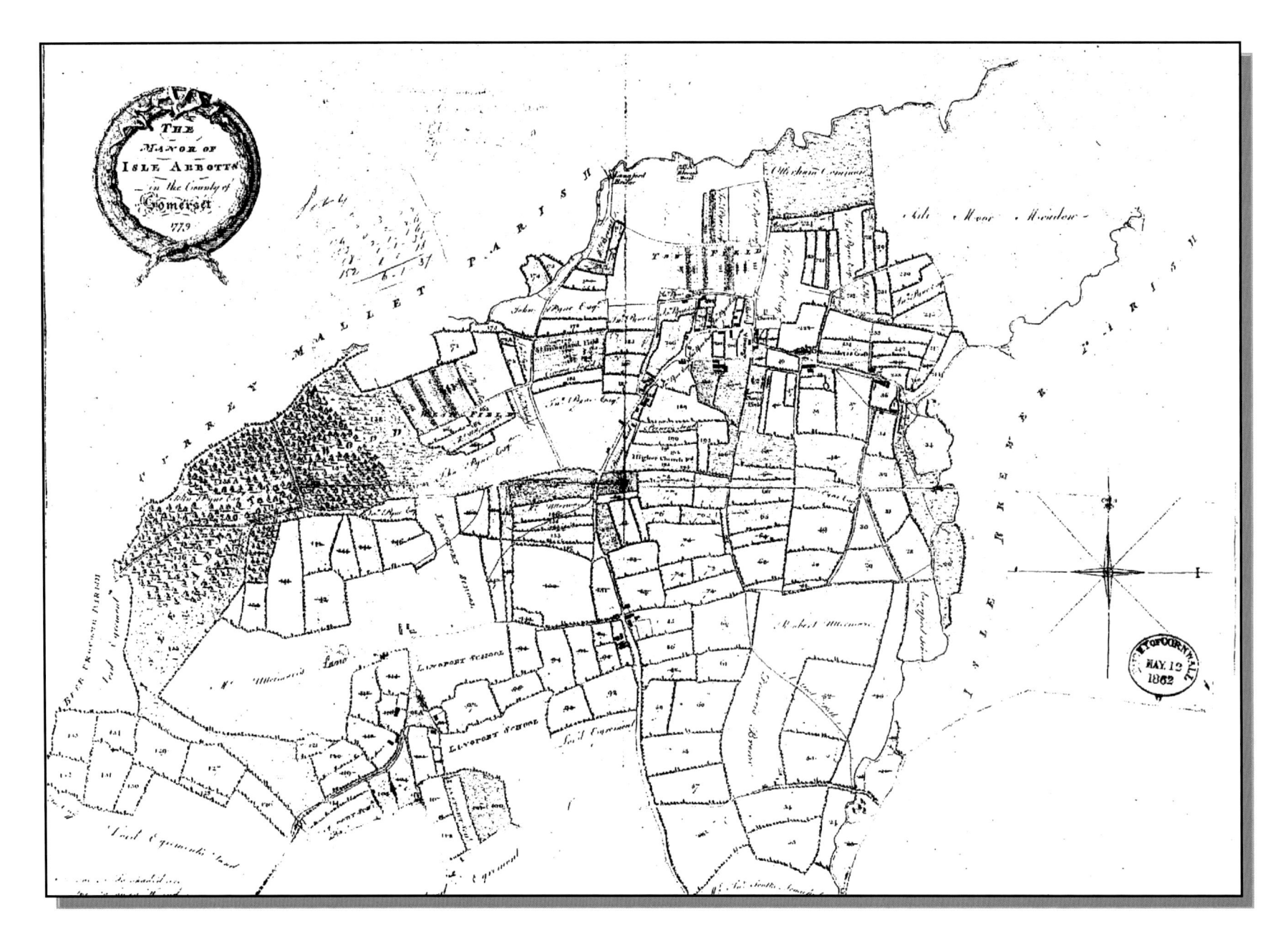

The earliest known detailed map of the village – 1779 – now in the archives of the Duchy of Cornwall
Note the large number of fields at that time and the strip field system in what was called then, as now, Town Field

Isle Abbots from the air, photographed in 1973

Above: Looking East

Right: Looking South

Overleaf: Looking West

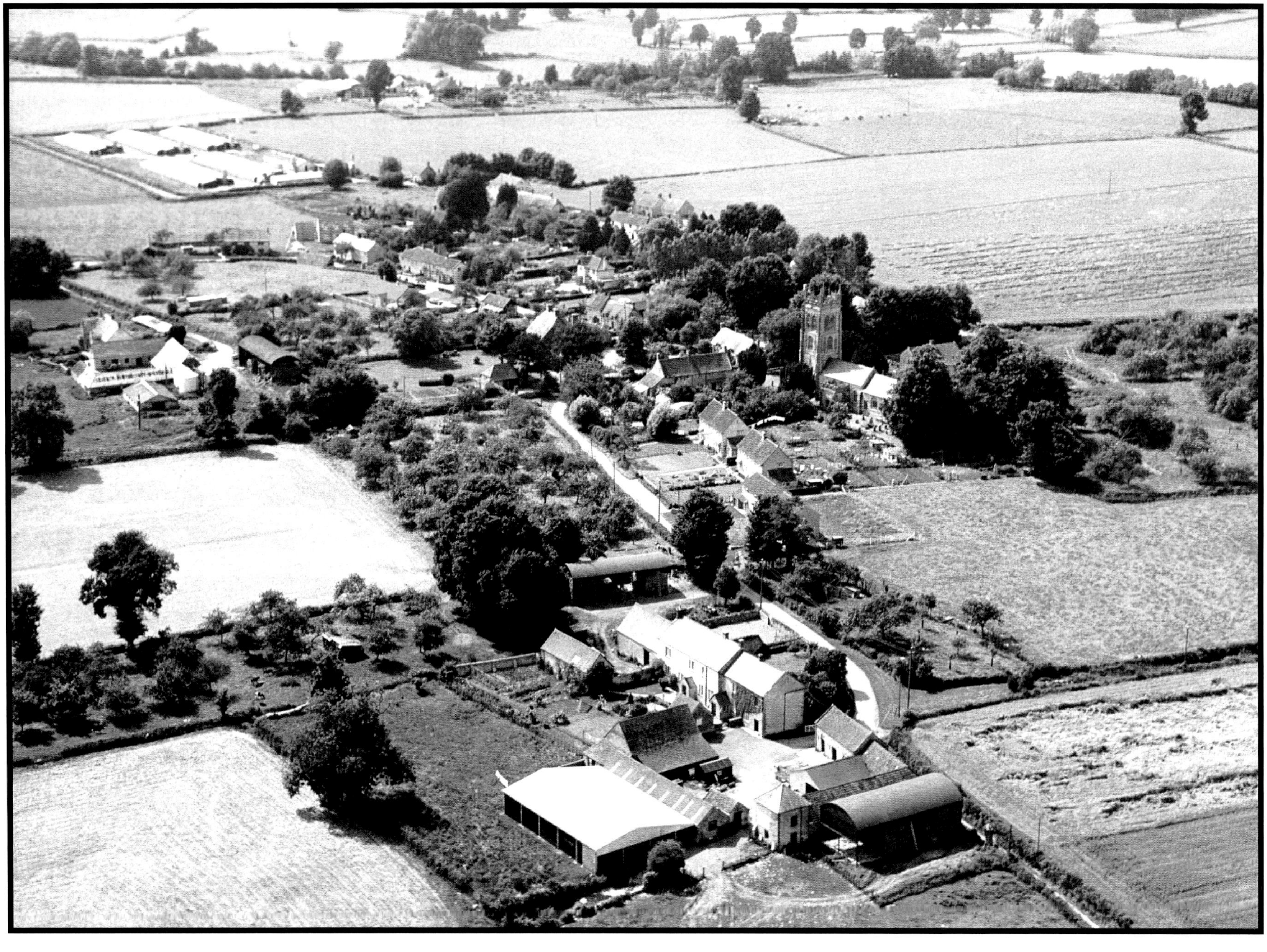

~~~ Housing: A Walk Around The Village: ~~~
Houses and some of their occupants

Looking back at copies of the Census it is sometimes difficult to decipher the names of some of the properties, as we know them today. The earliest Census was 1841 so information before that time is far more difficult to obtain. The Census officer did not always walk round the village in exactly the same order and his writing was not always very clear. The 1851 Census lists houses in the centre of the village as just 'Street' giving them a number as he went round. Some very small farms were swallowed up by the bigger farms and some cottages demolished, fallen down, converted into one house from two cottages or changed their names. Agricultural workers usually lived in a cottage tied to their employer. Some family names were very intertwined and the likes of Adams, Humphry and Patten for example appear frequently over the years. So this chapter will do its best to give a flavour of the houses and occupants at various times. The major farms and some of their cottages are covered in a chapter of their own.

So take an imaginary walk around the village, perhaps a hundred years ago, and picture life in the past. The weary farm labourers walking home at the end of a long day. The women busy in their homes washing, cooking and caring for their many children, as well as making gloves or sewing shirts. The young children playing in the fields and the older children going to school when they were not being given some other task to do. Neighbours meeting in the street on their way to the shops or to attend church or chapel or on the rare treat of going to market or to Taunton by horse and cart.

We begin our journey from the south of the village, coming from the Ilminster direction, passing Ashford and Woodlands farms and cottages mentioned in the farming chapter.

ROUNDOAK

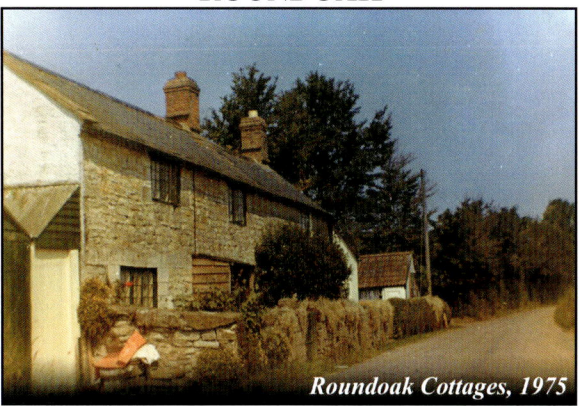

Roundoak Cottages, 1975

There once stood a group of four cottages on either side of the road at Roundoak. According to early census reports there were sometimes 5 or 6 cottages, so they must have been divided up at times. Ownership or tenancy changed over the years, but the names of Hooper the thatching family and Crocker, a mainly labouring family, are constantly repeated. However in 1841 John Crocker was described as a tailor and later his brother Samuel's son William was also a tailor. Over the years the various women in these cottages were glove makers, seamstresses or collar stitchers as well as looking after hungry large families of thatchers or agricultural workers. So this corner of the village must have been a hive of activity.

Isaac Hooper a thatcher aged 50, was described as residing in Roundoak north in 1841, living with his wife Sarah and sons Isaac aged 20 and daughter Mary 15 and Robert 15. John Bond only 10-years-old was a servant. By 1851 Mary was still living at home with her one-year-old son George. She had married a James Bond in 1848 and at George's baptism in 1850, his father was described as a soldier. Was this the same John Bond who had been living in the house as a servant?

By 1871 Isaac Hooper junior who was then 50 was a thatcher and shopkeeper but we do not know what he sold. His daughter Ellen made kid gloves. By 1881 the cottages were divided to provide for 6 families. Ann Grabham aged 69 who was a nurse lived alone in one part. Isaac and Harriet Hooper in another, and Robert Hooper thatcher with wife Jane and 6 children in another. Robert Faulkner, a ploughman and family in another. Joseph Crocker and wife Jane with 7 children in another. Their eldest daughter Ellen was described as a deaf imbecile. They had 2 sons who were ploughboys and 2 sons as agricultural labourers. Then another local name appears with Arthur Mears a labourer and wife Elizabeth a collar stitcher and their one-year-old son Charles.

Interestingly at the beginning of the 20th century Joseph Crocker who was now 73 had risen to a dairyman on his own account with his son Edwin as dairyman. His other son Henry was a Teasel grower.

Various Hoopers continued for some time then during the mid 1900s 2 of the cottages fell into disrepair and were flattened. *Edmund Dare remembered (2002) when he lived in one of these cottages as a small boy around 1935. It had a thatched roof and there was a well in the garden.* The two remaining cottages at one time housed Mr. Pickford who grew and delivered his vegetables around the village and a retired couple, Mr. and Mrs. Greenhalgh in the other. When the cottages were sold in the 1980s they were joined into one house and have been further extended since and called Round Oak Cottage.

BADBURY HOUSE

Badbury House, 1980

A thatched house, which was once divided into 2 cottages and housed farm labourers, mainly for Woodlands Farm. When James Melhuish a labourer, lived there in 1871 his wife Sarah was a glover together with looking after their 5 children and 2 lodgers. Neighbour Jemima Paul was also a glover. Charles Adams was a ploughman in 1881 and his wife a charwoman, and next-door James Lewis was listed as a shepherd. By 1911 Joseph Crocker's two daughters were shirtmakers with neighbours Susan Lawrence and Rose Davy making collars. So this was another very busy corner of the village.

BADBURY DAIRY HOUSE

This house, built in the 1600s, was once the house where the dairy manager for Bromes Farm lived. From the earliest census in 1841 Caroline Humphry was the dairywoman, living with her young children Sarah and Mary. However by 1851 Henry Humphry aged only 23 was listed as a farmer with 66 acres employing 8 men and 2 boys but dairyman was mentioned again by 1881 with Henry Collins, followed by William Parker 1891, Edwin Matravers in 1901 and William Clarke in 1911 with his assistant William Hughes. Having become detached from the farm many years ago, it has long been in private hands with several changes of ownership. There is a story that when Miss Salmons, a spiritualist, lived there in the 1960s, she removed all the inner doors to allow spirits to move freely. A new extension was added to this old thatched house in the early 21st century.

Badbury Dairy House, 1939; Mrs F. Adams

BADBURY BARTON

The house now called Badbury Barton was originally the dairy unit for Bromes Farm. In the 1970s Bill and Val Dresser converted the barns into a house. They built pig-rearing units on the land behind. The barns have been further extended by the current owners and the pig units removed to form a very pleasant garden..

During conversion, 1976

Badbury Barton 2002 Claire, Mike, Alexander & Samuel Smith

BADBURY BARN

Badbury Barn, 1986

This barn, which stands sideways on to the road, was converted to a private house in 1986 and has stayed in the same hands since.

LITTLE FLITTERS

This cottage now very much extended was the birthplace of Jack Adams born in 1907. He was the youngest of 3 brothers and a sister who died as a baby. The cottage was then called Garden Plot, which they called 'Under the Hill' because the ground behind the house rises slightly uphill and was divided into garden plots. It was then a 2-up 2-down cottage. There is a description in the 1911 Census of 'Rumpards Plot' 4 rooms, so this is probably the same dwelling. His father Henry was described as a Waggoner and brother Tom as a ploughboy.

The family moved across the road to Tysons. When Jack married Margaret (always known as 'Sis') they lived there with his family. They were still living there during the second world war when 2 evacuees came to stay before moving into a new council house in Manor Road. Sis preferred it at Tysons as there was more

Little Flitters, 1975

traffic going past and she got to know the sound of each vehicle or cart.

Edmund Dare was also born in this cottage in 1928. He only lived there until he was 3 but in 2002 could vividly remember the steps by the front door.

THE INN / TYSONS / CROSS CLOSE

1841 Census lists William Humphry as a publican along with his wife Sarah. 10 years later he was still the publican along with his wife and children William, Sarah, Robert, Mary, James and Charles and a lodger John Griffiths a Blacksmith. However, by 1861 the Inn was no longer and had turned into cottages known as Tysons. William was described as a farmer with 47 acres.

The Inn known as The Lamb (according to Jack Adams) was bought by Major Barrett a local landlord, and one time owner of Bromes Farm. It was let out as 2 cottages to agricultural workers, probably those working for him. These cottages were demolished and in the 1960s. Billy and Renee Bicknell built a house called Cross Close for their retirement from Bromes Farm and the property was sold after they had both died.

GREYSTONES

This bungalow was built by Mr and Mrs Jack Humphry to retire into from Manor Farm in 1957. The property had several tenants since, before being sold.

TWO STEPS
–How Mr James Norbury found it.
From an undated magazine article.

Two Steps, c1960's from magazine article

'When arriving with a friend at an estate agents in Crewkerne I asked in a casual chatty way, if he had a small cottage on his books. He told me of one, I told him the price was too high, to which he replied, "Well go along and see it and if you like it, make an offer."

We drove a few miles north of Ilminster passing through some of the loveliest scenery of the Somerset countryside, and then, round the bend in a narrow country lane, we found it. I got out of the car and rubbed my eyes, I didn't believe it. Here before us was the cottage of every picture postcard, of every country lovers dream. Neat and white and thatched, it stood there in a small overgrown garden and I knew that this must be ours, that here was a veritable answer to prayer.'

…… "We found Two Steps almost two years ago and we are still striving for that innate perfection that such a place demands. It is a home, a haven to live in, a quiet place to die in; what more can any one of us ask?"

James died at the age of 68 and his friend Tony Pegrum who shared the cottage with him sold it in 1973.

Mr Norbury was a retired chief designer for Patons and Baldwins Ltd. He was an expert on knitting and had written books and magazine articles on the subject. He made the shawl for Prince Andrew's christening. He made his first broadcast for the BBC in 1946 and subsequently built up a large following for his exposition of knitting patterns and techniques on television.

Mrs Joan Crisp who moved to Isle Abbots in 1955 told how her older half sister Eveline had moved into Two Steps, which she rented from the Habberfield family. It was previously called Rose Cottage but Eveline had renamed it Two Steps because it was an effort for her to climb the two steps from the road. Later some people who bred Pekinese dogs moved in and the dogs did a lot of damage to the Cobb walls.

This listed cottage built in the late 16th/early 17th Century seems to have changed hands a number of times. According to the 1841 census, this could be the cottage lived in by John Humphry age 67 a farmer, his wife Betty 65, Hannah 55, James 25. By 1851 it is listed as James aged 36 being head of the house, described as a farmer with 8 acres and no labourers. Hannah 45 and Jane 32 his sisters, listed as shopkeeper and assistant shopkeeper/ housekeeper.

Another well-known occupant of Two Steps was Peter Mayle who moved to France and wrote the book *'A Year in Provence'*.

WALDRONDS

Waldronds Old Barns 1983 showing the old School House beyond

Could this be another name for Two Steps as believed by some? Or was Waldronds another cottage on the site between Two Steps and the old school? It has always been understood that Waldrond was the butcher, there are references to quite a few members of that family in the Baptismal registers. The first mention of a butcher was in September 1765 when Jane the daughter of William (Butcher) and his wife Martha was baptized. The 1851 Census describes James Walrond (without the middle d) as being a butcher aged 59, his wife Mary a dressmaker, children George and Ann scholars. By 1861 George aged 20 was also a butcher. Until the present bungalows were built, there stood an open fronted barn on this site adjoining land belonging to Northalls Farm and always known as Waldronds. The barns were demolished in 1983 and now one of these bungalows is named Waldronds.

Three other bungalows were built on this site, known as **FRIARS FIELD**, **CROFTON** and **CELANDINE**. Across the road 2 more bungalows were built on either side of the old **MARSHES** bungalow, **DORA THEOS** and **MEADOWVIEW**

SCHOOL HOUSE

This was originally built to house the schoolteacher, and is attached to the school, (now the village hall). It has been in private ownership since the school closed in 1959.

HARVEST COTTAGE

Harvest Cottage, 2002: Mrs. Mary Powell

This house was once the village shop, and lived in by Kate Adams. The shop was known as Lanes as Miss Lane who rented the Old Manse worked there. Further information is given in the shopping chapter.

THE OLD MANSE

This cottage, which is set back from the road and almost joins the Chapel building, is reputed to have originally been lived in by Teasel growers. In 1841 the Census shows the occupants as Uriah and Sarah Foot and Alfred aged 4. Uriah was described as a 'Dissenting Minister'. By 1851 John Chapple, Baptist Minister lived there with his housekeeper Elizabeth Baker. In 1857 the chapel bought the house for £100. In 1901 the cottage was being rented out to Thomas Garland who together with his son Walter aged 15 were Teasel packers. His wife Sarah and daughter Lavinia were shirt makers. Son George aged 18, an agricultural labourer and 11-year-old Blanche a scholar. This family had previously lived at Uttermares. By 1950 Miss Lane, who had been a tenant of The Manse for many years, died. It was decided by the Chapel to sell the property and in 1951 it was sold at auction for £1000 and the money invested by the Chapel. Since then the cottage has been improved and has had several changes of ownership.

The Old Manse

CUFFS ORCHARD

This thatched house, probably dating from the late 16th Century, was presumably named after the original owner of the land. Early Census reports describes it as just Cuffs Part 1 and 2, when it was divided into units for 2 families. It would appear that these cottages were always let to farm workers, so either tied or rented out. The families were quite large and it must have been very crowded.

In 1841 Thomas and Betty Baker lived in one half with only 2 children. James and Mary Webb lived in the other with 7 children and a 14-year-old lodger who was also an agricultural labourer.

By 1861 there was Eli and Hannah Adams in one half, Hannah and daughter Emily 13 were both described as glovers. Charles, a ploughboy was aged 11, and Sarah was aged 9. In the other half was Harry Adams and wife Sarah with Mark, 18 a carpenters apprentice and Elizabeth, 14.

Eli Adams with extra children was still there in 1871 and joined next door by Samuel Hooper a carpenter.

There was a different Adams family by 1891 on one side and James Payne a ploughman in the other, along with wife Susan, Sidney 19 a labourer, Emily 18 a shirt maker, Charles, 12 a Ploughboy, Herbert 10, Lillie 8, and Percy 10 months.

The 1911 census describes one half of Cuffs as having 4 rooms housing the Payne family with 12 children. In the other half with 3 rooms lived Elizabeth Symes a widow, a shirt machinist living with her son William aged 20 a blacksmith, Maud 15 also making shirts, Ivy 7, Frederick 5 and Doris 3.

Peter Jacobson, now 90 and living in Australia remembered when he moved into Cuffs Orchard at the beginning of the Second World War. At that time it was rented by his father and Uncle Tom. The cottage intended for 8 people soon became filled by 21 but he said thank goodness for the magnificent bathroom and toilet with their mirrored ceilings, and the big Aga cooker, but no electricity! His sister Joan was married in Isle Abbots church to Norris, a Civil Pilot, in 1939.

The cottages were joined into one attractive large house and lived in by three sisters, the 'Miss Wilcox'. Frances Burgess remembered these formidable ladies hobbling through the village in their boots, always in black with big hats. They didn't speak to many people and children were in awe of them.

A Mrs. Hibberd followed them, and in 1968 Dr Geoffrey Gordon OBE and his wife Enid moved in. Dr Gordon died in 1980 but Enid stayed on for a few years before moving to be near her family in Cornwall. There have been several owners since then, each making improvements and taking care of the property. One of these was John and Pat Ferguson who took an

Cuffs Orchard 2002 John and Pat Ferguson

active part in the village with Pat as Church Secretary and John as Treasurer.

THE CHAPEL

After the chapel closed for services in December 2006, it was sold to Mary Temperley and Jake Motley who converted it to a splendid family home for themselves and their sons Phoenix, Rufus and Flynn.

COUNCIL HOUSES – 1 - 4 Ilton Road

The first 2 houses were built in 1935 and the Dare family moved into No.1, bringing up their 4 children. Ethel and Edmund Dare lived there until they died. Their son Edmund remembered moving from a thatched cottage at Roundoak, no longer there. His father came from Isle Brewers and worked at Ashford Mill and later as a carter for Mr Perrin. Edmund also helped cut teasels from the age of 12. His grandfather walked from Stoke St. Gregory to learn the milling trade at Isle Brewers Mill.

Edmund (junior) was born in 1928. He remembered seeing the fire engine bringing water from the river at Two Bridges to put out the fire at the thatched cottages near Colliers, and seeing a steam lorry from Kings of Bishops Lydeard at Roundoak and Edgar Habberfields' first car, a canvas topped Vauxhall. He remembered Vetches, Trefolium, Chaff, Mangolds, and Linseed Cake, which came from the miller, Bill Dampnett of Barrington. He moved to Barrington when he married in 1947.

The Adams family moved into No.2. Herbert Charles Adams, known as Harry had been born in the village and left school aged 12 and worked on a farm until he joined the Great Western Railway engineering department. He later worked as a stoker in a local nursery for 26 years until he lost his leg in a motorcycle

Harry Adams making corn dollies

accident. He married Lily Sutton in 1927 and they had 4 children, Ron, Brenda, Lorna and Phyllis.

Harry loved working in his shed making toys like whistles, dancing dolls and corn dollies. After his accident he made cane items for sale. He was an avid reader and spoke the old Somerset dialect. He loved to tell stories and sing traditional folk songs and played the Melodeon and Mandolin Harp. He died aged 79 in 1982. Lily succeeded him by some years.

No 3 Ilton Road, 2002, home of Brenda Innes

When it became vacant, daughter Brenda moved into No.3 next door with her husband Jim Innes who she met when he was in the air force at Merryfield. They had one daughter, Charmaine. Brenda had many tales to tell of growing up in Isle Abbots. She remembered as a child how the water was pumped from a well and lighting in the house was by oil lamps. She lived there alone after Jim died in 1998 until moving into a sheltered bungalow in Langport where she died in 2012.

Next-door at No.4 lived the Tapp family. Henry and Mrs Tapp moved there when it was first built. Henry worked as a blacksmith at Colliers and then in India as a blacksmith in the army during the war. They had five children, their daughter Phyllis married Bill Burton who worked at Northalls Farm and Evelyn married Mr Slade and lived in No.3. Their son Don was born in 1918 in Harvest Cottage. As a young man he sometimes pumped the organ in church for the organist Miss Higgins. He left school at 14 and worked at Northalls Farm for 25 years and later for Dick Lucas at his farm buildings at Ashford, mainly with chickens. Don's father had died and his mother died just before he married Phyllis Derrick in 1954. The newlyweds lived in No.4 along with Don's aunt Annie Derrick.

Phyllis, who had been brought up in Wrantage remembered that when she first moved into the house there was a furnace in the kitchen that was heated by a coal fire to provide water for the downstairs bathroom. Both Phyllis and Aunt Annie worked at home making gloves. The materials were brought to them from a factory in Taunton. To make a pair of ordinary leather gloves they were paid 2/6d. They also made fur gloves and fine kid gloves, which were more difficult because of the fine stitching.

Phyllis also worked as a Home Help for the 3 Misses Wilcox who lived next door at Cuffs Orchard. She did not really like that job very much. Later she also went to clean for Mrs Trimble at the Old Vicarage when she took in foreign students and then as a B&B.

Don and Phyllis did not have any children and she lived alone in the house for some time after Don died and then moved to a sheltered bungalow in Curry Mallet in 2001.

THE RUINS / WILLERSLEY

On the site where Willersley now stands was a former cottage lived in by the Cotty family in 1841 and quite possibly many years before when William, then 65, was described as a farmer. By 1861 his son James was a farmer with 48 acres employing 3 men and 1 boy. By 1871 the property was listed as Copses where James lived with wife Mary, but by 1881 the property was listed as Borough. The cottage is believed to have burnt down and known locally as 'The Ruins'.

This plot became the property of Mr Harry Priddle who kept pigs there. It was sold to developers in 1972 and described as being over ¾ acre, with dilapidated stone built stable, galvanised shed, well and iron hand pump thereon. The completed house was sold to Mr and Mrs Smith-West in 1974, who named it Willersley. In 1988 it changed hands again and was purchased by John and Elaine Guest who brought up their 3 children there. Elaine is an active member of the village, having been Village Hall Chairman, Parish Clerk and Churchwarden.

COX'S PIT

This large ditch was previously a much bigger pond. It is not sure how it got its name but is probably a derivation of either Copses from the nearby cottage or from the Cottys who lived there.

CLOSEFIELDS

This cottage was built about 1800 for the Guardians of the Poor of the Langport Union as three houses. It was sold in 1840 for £40 to John Patten, described as "three cottages under one roof with six perches of garden".

Robert Lee became part owner for the sum of £30 in 1856 who then sold it to Emma Lee in 1870 for £7 as an outstanding mortgage payment. 1874 sees it being sold again to James Cottey for £50 and to his niece Emma Patten for 10/- in 1879.

Sold again in 1931 (twice), and in 1932 when it was known as Chestnuts. More sales in 1934 and 1938 when it was known as Closefields Cottage and in 1939 to Mr and Mrs Oswald Little for the sum of £962.10/-. This family stayed rather longer, until 1948. Then Guy Manning Stewart-Wallace and Gilbert Scott-Eames purchased it jointly for £5000. When Scott-Eames died

Closefields, c.1940

his wife Rose married Emanuel Verduin in 1965 and they lived there until 1978, when it was purchased by Ann Trimble, and in 1983 by Dorothy Gardner.

Phyllis Tapp reminisced how her husband Don once told her of a Mr. Sealey who lived at Closefields. He had a donkey and made a shed for it out of old orange boxes. Rumour had it that the donkey fell down the well and died!

Closefields has known many residents and the cottage has changed dramatically over the years. Then in 1996 Peter and Pauline Herbert purchased it. After Pauline died Peter continues to live there and take part in village activities and always willing to lend a hand with any little jobs for his neighbours.

WICKEN / ROSELANDS

A piece of land next to Closefields belonging to Northalls Farm was sold in 1972 and a house built on it. Mrs Barbara Wright moved in and called it Wicken. She lived there until 1990 taking an active part in the village and particularly as Churchwarden. (Further references to Barbara are in the Church chapter). The current owners have changed the name to Roselands.

LAUREL COTTAGE

Laurel Cottage is believed to have been built as two small cottages in approximately 1730. There was an indenture and releases in 1761 between Churchill Rose and his wife Betty of Netherbury Dorset and William Wimbridge of Abbots Ile, husbandman and Daniel Collingdon of Beaminster, gent. For the consideration of £10. Churchill Rose sold to Will. Wimbridge and his heirs all that messuage and dwelling house with the garden, orchard and backside, by estimation half a rood lying in Abbots Ile, then in the tenure and occupation of Mary Chick.

We know from the Church Poor Book that Mary Chick was the recipient of help through her brother James Baker "she being lowsey".

Laurel Cottage with a former resident

In 1819 Richard Wimbridge inherited the house and the tenant was James Paul. It then passed to Joshua Crocker whose wife Mary was related to Samuel Tapp who appeared to own 'The Laurels'. In 1901 it was still housing two agricultural workers and their families and was joined into one house sometime after that date and gradually extended.

In 1930 it was sold to Walter Somers and appears to have changed hands 7 times until the present owners purchased it in the 1980s.

Thimble Hall 2002: John, Pam and Andrew Medcalf in the back garden

THIMBLE HALL

This house, previously called Applegarth was built in 1975 in part of the garden of Lumbards House when it belonged to Miss Elsie Brooks. She only wanted to build a bungalow but planners insisted on a house so she just lived downstairs. Applegarth retained most of the land that belonged to Lumbards. Unfortunately she did not live in it for very long before passing away. The house was then sold to Len and Pat Harden and then to John and Pamela Medcalf.

LUMBARDS HOUSE

This house, which still retains its thatch, was first constructed around 1620 with later additions. The name of Thomas Lumberd is mentioned in the Muster Role of 1569, so it is possible the house took the family name. The 1842 tithe map describes the site of only 0.2 acres as Rumpits Plot, owned and occupied by Thomas Lumbard. However a Thomas and his wife and two children lived at church cottages in 1841 and a John Lombard with wife and four children appeared to live at Cuffs Orchard ten years later. During 1851 3 of these children were buried in the churchyard. The house was

Lumbards House: David, Jackie simon and Tom Jay and Jackie's mother, Mary

listed in 1861 as being in 2 parts occupied by James Smith a blacksmith on one side and William Vile in the other. Samuel Betty, a Carpenter and John Walden, an agricultural labourer, followed them later. As the house still has 2 staircases, one at either end, this is quite possible to imagine.

Henry Taylor c.1920

By the beginning of the 20th century Lumbards was occupied by just one family. Henry and Caroline Taylor lived there with just 3 of their children, which by the 1911 census had increased to 7. There had also been 5 other infants that had died. Henry Junior was a ploughboy at the age of 16, and sadly was killed at the beginning of World War 1 (further details in the war chapter). His father died in 1927 aged sixty.

The house and land, by then known as Lumbards Plot, which until then had belonged to Northalls Farm, was sold in 1930, and purchased by Miss Passavant. Caroline Taylor moved to Wellings Farmhouse. The house was sold again in 1949 to Miss Brooks. Around this time the name was changed to Cherry Tree Cottage. Miss Brooks built a house in the grounds called Applegarth (now Thimble Hall).

Pamela and Randall Davis and family moved into Lumbards in 1975, when it was still known as Cherry Tree Cottage. After several other changes the house reverted to being called Lumbards when purchased by David and Jackie Jay in 2001 along with their sons Simon, Tom and Jackie's mother Mary.

By a chance conversation between David and Jackie and a lady called Muriel about moving to Lumbards she said, "that must be my grandparents' house. My mother was born there and I used to spend my summer holidays there and walk across the fields to Curry Mallet with my grandma to have her hats made." Muriel must have been a granddaughter of Henry and Caroline Taylor.

ABBOTS GLEN
This bungalow was built in 1970 by Bill Clarke for his own occupation for a while and has changed hands several times since then.

GREENHATCH
This old cottage was once known as Townsfield or Townsend Cottage. The field behind it being known today as Townfield.. By 1891 it was occupied by Richard Salway a carpenter, and his wife Eliza and 5 children. By 1911 it was divided between Richard and Eliza and 2 adult children and Henry and Mrs Tapp. Richard was then known as a carpenter and wheelwright so presumably worked for the Tapps at Colliers. Eliza was a shirt maker.

A delightful tale of finding Greenhatch by Emily Akers has been given to the present owners Helen and Danny Evans. It was written in the form of a letter to Emily's daughter Winifred (known as Pat).

"It has a very old front door with a window either side which I think I can camouflage and alter, but the beams are really lovely in both downstairs rooms. The living room, which the front door opens into, has a lobby leading off looking over the adjoining cornfield, which I fancy for writing and some of my books. The original fireplace has been removed and replaced with a modern Devon type with a plain oak mantel. There is a small dining room, papered with quite the most hideous wallpaper, but not too bad a size.

Leading out of the sitting room there is a door to the staircase. There is a wee landing on top and a tiny window looking onto the back garden. There are three bedrooms. Fine, lofty rooms and although two of the

GREENHATCH ISLE ABBOTTS Price: £65/75,000 1991
Requiring refurbishment, entrance porch, 3 reception rooms, kitchen, rear hall, bathroom, 3 bedrooms. Large garden, car parking. Ref:
(Newspaper sales advertisement)

rooms share one window, having originally been one very large room, they are both light and airy. The middle room has a little four-cornered porthole looking over the meadows and garden at the back, like a little sort of niche.

The thatch is old but in fair condition. There is a small kitchen and two sheds. There is the original 'little hut' halfway down one side of the garden, but so overgrown with ivy that it is quite pretty and I should leave it.

There is some interesting plaster carving along the wall of the sitting room; just a simple design, with rose, shamrock and thistle alternating in each scroll.

The well is just by the front door with an incredibly old iron lid to it, not very safe. We have one leaded window upstairs, the others being ordinary casement windows it makes the cottage look all cock-eyed." (Abridged version)

Daughter Marjorie thought the house was purchased in 1930/31 but deeds indicate a conveyance to E. Akers for 1943, so maybe it was rented to them before then. The youngest children Bill and Marjorie both attended the village school. Marjorie is in a school photo of 1935. Elder daughter Phyllis moved in with her mother and went to work on a farm nearby. Nothing much is mentioned about Mr Akers but after he died Emily sold the cottage in 1951 to Major J Felton who kept pigs on the adjoining land.

The cottage and land was then purchased by Mr Goff of South West Chicks, who erected the chicken rearing sheds and let out the cottage. The house was sold again separately in 1991 and underwent considerable alterations, including removing the thatched roof. The old decorative plaster frieze had been removed in earlier decorations in 1974. It then passed to the present owners.

STONEFORD

A recently built stone house built for the owners of the adjoining poultry raising unit.

COLLIERS

Built in the early 16th Century, this house with its jointed crucks has seen many changes. We first pick up the name of Colliers in the 1841 census when Abraham Tapp and wife Sarah and their 4-month-old son James lived there. Edward Hyder Brown then owned the house, barn and orchard.

Abraham was a machinist employing 3 men and 1 boy by the 1850s, making and repairing farm implements. The business grew and he trained his own son Robert to succeed him. By the 1880s Robert was employing 16 men and 3 boys. By the 1890s Elizabeth had born him 10 children and one of these, Samuel, became the manager of this thriving business after his father died.

The family gradually dispersed from the village but in 1951 Robert E. Tapp wrote to the vicar from America and his letter was published in the church magazine.

..."Although my days, for more than half a century, have been spent far from those quiet precincts, the fact remains that I was born almost in the shadow of the church tower, in the house of my father's 'Colliers' which had sheltered the family since the beginning of the nineteenth century, it also being the birthplace of my grandfather, the youngest child of his generation, in 1815. My parents reared a large family (a baker's dozen). Eleven survived and the first to go in World War 1. Eight now survive, and live in England except the youngest, a brother in Vancouver, and myself".

Tapps Agricultural Machinists at Colliers

In my day the names Tapp and Isle Abbotts were practically synonymous. …It is purely a case of nostalgia, a desire once more to get a letter with the old familiar postmark, which (again in my day) would have been affixed, or imprinted by one of the Misses Patten. ….My contacts have been few and far between, and I sometimes wonder who is toasting his toes in "our" old chimney corner or who is eating the apples from Paul's Orchard or at the Barrington's, Badbury or Woodlands?

It is difficult to visualise this old place without the personalities who once dominated the scene."

Colliers was purchased in 1925 by Major John Claude Steele where he brought up his son John. When Major Steele was serving in the Army in India he let out the property to a Mr Garl. On retiring from the army Major Steele took up a job in Taunton and would drive there in his chain driven Trojan car. John joined the Royal Air Force and rose to the ranks of Squadron Leader, serving in Cyprus and the Far East. He married his first wife Ann who lived in nearby Greenhatch and they

Tapps Agricultural Machinists at Colliers

Tapps exhibiting at a country show

Major Claude Steele leaning on "Dilly Cart"
belonging to Edgar Habberfield, outside Colliers on the right. Thatched cottage called Southview behind.

Colliers c.1970

brought up their two daughters at Colliers.

John loved to ride and hunt and once had a beautiful large white horse called Dolly. He was active in the purchase and restoration of the village hall and chairman of the Parish Council for many years until he died in 2001.

His widow Sue still lives in the house. The remains of the old Forge still exist and the old smithy shed across Blind Lane remains.

Sqn Ldr John Steele on Dolly

Samel Tapp the blacksmith outside the forge

HARVARDS / WAYSIDE COTTAGES - Glenfields and Weatheroak.

There were originally three modest cottages known as either Harvards (after that family who lived in one of them for many years) or Wayside Cottages. Originally they were part of Northalls Farm, which owned the field behind called Yawnfield, now known as Townfield and part of the Pyne estate.

Gradually the cottages were sold off privately but a terrible fire destroyed both the western and middle cottages. Mrs. Bennett who owned the middle cottage sold her ruins to Mr William Clarke of Church Street in 1942 for just £10. This middle cottage had been known as Southview. In 1943 Mr. Clarke then purchased the westernmost cottage from a Mr Fox and finally the intact cottage, then known as Harvards Cottage.

Wedding of Albert Adams and Nellie Crocker, 7/11/1912
Outside their first home at Wayside Cottages

Wayside Cottages before the fire, c.1930

Mr Clarke let out this cottage during the rest of 1940s and 50s. Then sometime in the 1950s he built a new cottage called Weatheroak and reconstructed and extended the easternmost part calling it Goldwell Cottage. In 1961 Goldwell was sold and again in 1962 to Ethel Anderson of Lane Cottage, Isle Abbots for £2,975. Mrs Anderson then sold it back to Mr Clarke in 1973 for £11,200 for his own use along with his wife Gertrude. After Bill Clarke died in 1985 his widow sold the house now known as Glenfields to a Mr Jones who in turn sold it to the present owners, David and Leslie Sutcliffe in 1987.

Both Glenfields and Weatheroak have been extended since the original rebuild.

The following story was supplied by Jan Ford now living in Canada and gives a vivid record of the cottage where she first lived. She was born in hospital in 1947 as the cottage was deemed unsuitable for a home birth as it only had a ladder to the bedroom.

"In 1946 my parents Geoff and Betty Ford were starting their married life and found a condemned cottage "Wayside" in Isle Abbots which cost half a crown a week. It had earth and straw walls. Their house was part of a terrace of houses, part of which had fallen down. It had one room upstairs and one room downstairs plus an extra kitchen room at the side. The landlord charged seven shillings and sixpence for the garage, far more than for the house itself. With the landlord's permission, Geoff wired the house for electricity and built a water heater out of a metal dustbin and installed an electric cooker. They had a tin bath which drained into the garden and a chemical toilet which had to be emptied in a hole in the garden." The family moved to Kent soon after Jancis was born.

Wayside Cottage, 1946

AVALON

This bungalow was built in 1974 at the bottom of the garden of Monks Cottage when owned by Mr & Mrs Grey. They moved in on their retirement from running the post office and shop but it has changed hands several times since. It is approached from Blind Lane.

UTTERMARES

This pair of cottages may have connections with the vicar, Rev James Uttermare who was in office from 1734. Records show that Robert and Honor Uttermare who lived somewhere in the village had a daughter Mary baptised in St Mary's church in 1742. Then

Uttermares before renovation - 2002

followed two more Uttermare baptisms, Elizabeth in July 1767 and buried in January 1768, followed by another Elizabeth in 1769.

The 1842 Tithe map shows that a Thomas and William Uttermare owned a lot of land in the parish that was let to other farmers but he did not seem to live in the village.

Starting from the 1841 census there is a long list of agricultural labourers living in the two cottages called Uttermares. Thomas and Ann Lumbard, a prominent name in the village lived in one half, and John Malewis and family occupied the other half of the cottages. By 1861 Frederick and Justina Kitch lived there, before moving to Dangards, and next-door Robert Hooper the thatcher with his wife Jane and 5 children and 11-year-old Thomas Taylor a thatcher's apprentice. By 1871 there were 10 Hooper children, which must have made it very crowded and 4 daughters next door with James and Ruth Alford.

All change again by 1891 when William and Sarah Woolmington and family lived on one side and on the other Thomas Garland, a Teasel packer, his wife Sarah and 5 children before they moved on to The Manse.

The cottages became owned by Northalls Farm and used for their workers. One couple that lived there for many years were Phyllis and Bill Burton. Phyllis

Uttermares~ Mrs Burton amongst the cabbages, 1973

cleaned at Colliers whilst Bill worked on the farm. Bill grew lots of vegetables in the front garden until he died in 1985. Phyllis was often seen around the village on her bicycle (see shopping chapter) almost up to the time of her death in 1991. The cottages continued to be let until they were inherited by Wendy Richards (nee Habberfield) and her son Alistair and have been modernised and extended.

CHURCH COTTAGE

Church Cottage 2002: Geoff & Emily Colenso, Ross and Ella

It is difficult to work out the sequence of residents of this cottage. Early census recorders often just listed anything near the church as 'Church Square'. But suffice it to say that most people were farm workers. Originally two cottages sharing one front door and divided by a passage from front to back.

The cottage was owned by Woodlands Farm and lived in by Jim Mead their carter and wife Ivy who was a servant. Then for many years Reg. and Frances Adams and their family rented it. When Frances died, Geoff and Emily Colenso purchased the cottage.

ABBOTS COTTAGE

It seems very likely that in 1841 this was the cottage lived in by Richard Patten a Shoemaker, together with wife Mary and 6 children. Still there in 1851 with 7 children with both mother Mary and daughter Mary aged 9 making gloves. Daughter Sophia aged 22 was described as a pauper and two sons as Agricultural labourers.

Before moving to Homestill in 1942 the house was lived in by Tom and Mary (Polly) Derrick with children Sidney, Kathleen, Mary and Frances along with Granny Mrs Elizabeth Crocker. They kept pigs and chickens in the back garden. Mr. Derrick worked on a pig farm at Isle Brewers and then became a roadman covering Isle Abbots and around. The family would often go for a walk on Sundays and he would eye up all the ditches and hedges that needed attending to. Mrs Derrick helped out at the Vicarage and made children's pyjamas on a sewing machine at home and these were collected on a Thursday afternoon. Gran used to wash and iron the church surplices to earn a few pence. These were starched and ironed with flat irons, which were lined up in front of the fire. The children all went to the village school until the age of 14. At that time Mr Bicknell from Bromes Farm owned the cottage.

In 1955 Patrick and Joan Crisp moved into Abbots

Abbots Cottage, 1920: Tom & Polly Derrick with Sidney & Kathleen

- 75 -

Polly Derrick at the back of the cottage

Cottage because Patrick liked the area when he had been stationed at Merryfield. Patrick wanted to start a nursery and they purchased the orchard attached to Monks Orchard. They put up some greenhouses at home and in the orchard and grew all sorts, bedding plants, tomatoes, vegetables, fruit and Strawberries. Unfortunately the nursery didn't provide a living and Pat went back to work. Joan carried on running the nursery for many years until selling the land back to the owners of Monks Orchard. They also had a little orchard in Woodlands Lane and put up chicken sheds to rear 200 chicks, and another for egg laying, they also kept bees on this land. Joan would cycle there every morning to look after the livestock.

Joan's music abilities came in very useful when she became the church organist. This was a task she performed devotedly for over 40 years along with taking part in all other church activities. Joan took over the chairmanship of the Friendship Club in 1969 and held this post for many years. Patrick died in 1986 and Joan lived in Abbots Cottage for the rest of her life until she died in 2008.

Geoff and Emily Colenso who owned Church Cottage next door then purchased the cottage. After considerable renovation they moved in and let out Church Cottage.

THE OLD VICARAGE

As far back as 1613 the Vicar of Isle Abbots complained of the tenants in 'the little Vicarage House'. It would seem that the Vicar was not always resident in the village and the property rented out. The Cotty family occupied the 'Parsons Cottage' in 1807. Then a family by the name of Burrows lived there between 1851 and 1871 but had disappeared from the village by 1881.

William Burrow was a Tailor and his wife Alice the schoolmistress in 1851. Their children Alice, Thomas, Mary, William, Rosa Ann, Henry, John and John Henry were all baptised in the church. John was buried aged 9 months.

The family then owned a Tailors shop in Bristol and several of the children worked there, including Rosa Ann the Grandmother of Mrs Bate who in 1996 recalled memories of her family told to her as a child. She said that the family lived in the Vicarage as the Vicar was a single man and it was too big for him and she remembers her Great Grandfather played the Cello there. The last person living there was the church caretaker before the building was pulled down to make room for a new vicarage around 1894.

The present 'Old Vicarage' was built during the time that the Rev. J. H. Taylor was in office between 1895 and 1907. Rev. Wilfred Probert was the last Vicar to reside there before it was sold for private use around 1960 and it has changed hands several times since then.

The Old Vicarage, 1911

VANGUARDS / DANGARDS MANOR ROAD

These cottages mentioned in the 1841 census are not given a name until 1861 when they are described as Dampards. They stood close to the road where the front gardens of the council houses are today. The 4 cottages seem to change their number of rooms according to the census but all the occupants were involved in farming of some kind, agricultural labourers, waggoners, a threshing machine feeder and sawyer. The sons also went on the farm at an early age. The women were mostly glovers even as young as 9. Some described as making shirts, a dressmaker and a washerwoman.

By 1871 they are called Dangards Pt. 1-4 and then in 1881 Vangards, and back to Danyards in 1911 at which time they seem to be in 3 parts, two having 4 rooms and one 5 rooms. In 1901, Arthur and Elizabeth Mear and their 9 children lived in one cottage. One can only imagine how crowded these cottages must have been.

The Dight family, in various combinations, lived in one cottage for many years. Starting in 1841 Mark aged 47 was a Mason, his wife Amelia 52 and son John 22. By 1851 Mark and Amelia are alone and she is described as a stay maker. At another cottage nearby son John is head of the house, also a Mason, with wife Rachel a glover and children Thomas 5 and Cornelius 1. By 1861 John was a widower and back at Dampards with sons Mark 14 and Cornelius 9 both agricultural labourers. Young Cornelius was buried in 1869.

By 1871 Mark aged 26 was head and an agricultural labourer. Married to Emily with children Esther 3, Cornelius 1 and John one month. Poor Emily was a widow by 1881 and described as a charwoman, Hester at 13 a servant and Annie aged 12 a scholar.

By the time Emily was 43 she was supporting herself as a Post woman and letter carrier, and lived with her 21-year-old daughter Annie, who made shirts and granddaughter Mabel aged 3. Annie Dight was also known to be a post woman so she must have taken over from her mother at some time.

In one of the other cottages in the row in 1871 Frederick Kitch agricultural labourer lived with his wife Justina a glover and 4 children. Justina was also a washerwoman for nearby Manor Farm.

In 1938 the land on which these cottages stood was sold to the Langport District Council and four substantial council houses built lying back from the road.

Jack and Sis Adams moved into one of these new houses, No 4, and lived there for the rest of their lives. Sissie made gloves at home. Jack went to work at Bromes Farm at the age of 13 and then worked for Harry Humphry at Woodlands Farm in 1927, which is when he started driving milk lorries. His lorry, a Morris Commercial, had only the bottom half of a door and was cold in winter; it did not have any windscreen wipers. He remembered carrying milk churns across the field to the lorry when it was flooded in Beercrocombe. He delivered milk to Waldrons Park in Isle Brewers for making cheese and to Thorney.

One day Jack was invited to a party at the Maddison's House in Fivehead and went without his parents at the age of 10. The tables were laid with free cigarettes for the adults, but he smoked so many it made him ill. His mother did not know why he was so ill all night and threatened to call the doctor next morning, but he managed to get up and go to school and had never smoked since.

Jack remembered that when he was young the doctor was Dr Verekar from Curry Rivel and he thought he was the image of King Edward VII. He came to the village on Mondays and Thursdays, first on a motorbike and then in a Ford car with only 2 gears. If you needed a doctor urgently Isle Abbots post office would telegraph to the Maddisons at Fivehead who would get a message somehow to Curry Rivel. Then came Dr Glover also from Curry Rivel but he was killed at the bottom of Mile Hill, Fivehead in a car accident whilst out on a call.

Reg and Winnie Burgess

Next-door at No.3 lived Reginald and Winifred Burgess (Reg. and Winnie) along with their children Heather and Richard who went to the village school. When Heather married she moved to Devon. Richard went to work at Manor Farm. Winnie spent her later life confined to a wheelchair and died in 1992. Reg. had been born at one of the pair of brick cottages at Southey Farm across the river (which now have been demolished). When he left school he first went to work at Manor Farm. Reg. then worked as a nurseryman for 27 years before his retirement. His duties included maintaining the boilers and this had led to his death of Asbestosis. In their younger healthier years they had joined in village activities. Among other things, Reg. can be remembered as giving generous glasses of Sherry to the Carol Singers! The house has continued to be lived in by Richard Burgess.

House 1 and 2 Manor Road have had various residents and No. 2 has been lived in by John and Vivienne Patch for many years and is now owned by them.

CONIFERS AND GLEBE HOUSE

Next to the sight of the four council houses in Manor Road a piece of land called Samuels was sold to build two new properties Glebe House and The Conifers in 1976.

PITTS COTTAGE

The date stone on the end of this cottage is 1583. It is presumed named after former residents of the Pitt (or Pytt) family of whom there were many. However there are earlier references to the family in the baptism registers for Isle Abbots. The baptisms are for Johanna in 1562, Agnes? 1565, and Jane 1568, all daughters of John Pytt. There are various references to this family in the 16th century. Certainly from the first census the building has been divided into two cottages that lay very close to the River Isle and must have suffered frequent flooding.

Like most cottages, agricultural workers would have lived in them.

In 1841 and 1851 they were lived in by the Winter and Winnil family. By 1861 there was a Thomas Mitchell listed as Shepherd. 1871 Abraham and Sarah Mear along with seven children. The name Mear appears frequently in the village. Another Shepherd Thomas Evans in 1881, presumably looking after the flocks at Manor Farm. By 1891 the name Chorley first appears with Benjamin a ploughman and his wife Sarah and 3 children. By 1901 Benjamin has a second wife Rosa along with 4 children and a stepdaughter, whilst 3-year-old Lucy Chorley is shown as a lodger with the Symes family next door who only have a 9 year old daughter Beatrice.

The 1911 census describes Pitts as 5 rooms with the Chorley family, now only Lillian, William and Lucy 13 back home, and 4 rooms with the Symes family. Daughter Beatrice aged 19 is interestingly listed as working in a shirt factory rather than at home like many ladies at that time. Lucy became a teacher and Anthony Habberfield remembers that when Isle Abbots School closed, Miss Chorley was teaching at Hatch Beauchamp and would take him and his sister Wendy to school in her Austin 7 with leather seats.

In 1974 the portion nearest the river was still lived in by Mrs Manning before it was considered unfit and left empty. Sidney and Violet Harris and their grandson Kevin occupied the other cottage until they moved into their council house, 1 Ilton Road.

The cottages owned by the Duchy Manor Farm were due for demolition in 1986 but this decision was reprieved and in 1989 they were modernised into one attractive house that is rented out.

MONKS THATCH

Believed to be of 15/16th century origins, this pretty cottage with title deeds dating from 1798 and mentioning the name of Richard Illot could have been called Church Hatch. The house was probably built long before that date. When sold in 1818, records show that it had been let to William Illot for a term of 500 years. Some say it may have been the Priests House at one time but there is no real evidence for this.

It is very difficult to trace past residents of this house, which is on the corner opposite the church. The census reports varied and all the cottages near the church were sometimes listed as Church Hatch, Church Corner or Church Square. In 1871 listings were for Church Square 1-7, so one of these would have been Monks Thatch. The occupants were listed as labourers, journeyman, blacksmith, mason, superannuated ex P.C., seamstress, dressmaker and a nurse.

Mr & Mrs Hunt left the house in 1977 after living there for 7 years and Derold Page and Monty Ashman bought it. Monty has since died but Derold continues to live there.

Pitts Cottage

Monks Thatch, 2002: Derold Page with Anya

ABBOTS ORCHARD

This house was built for Colonel John and Mrs Evelyn Stevens on land belonging to Monks Orchard. John and Evelyn were friends of the Murphy's who owned the land and purchased it from them. The house was designed with a wing for Evelyn's elderly parents. Both John and Evelyn were very active members of the church, parish council and village hall. They were always available to help or lend a listening ear. After John retired from the army he was appointed Wessex area organiser for the Save The Children Fund in 1977 working from his home. When the large garden at Abbots Orchard became a burden they moved to a bungalow in Fivehead and Abbots Orchard then changed hands twice with the current owners extending the property.

MONKS COTTAGE

This was originally 2 cottages. The southern, smaller, part was at one time the village shop and post office.

View from the Church Tower 1966 showing Monks Cottage; Monks Orchard beyond, with nursery in between

c.1940's: Now Monks Cottage

C.1900 postcard showing what is now Greggs, The Old Bakehouse, Talata Cottage and 2 Church Street

MONKS ORCHARD

This house was built in the 1930s and lived in by Charles and Beatrice Jobling and their daughter Biddy. Miss Jobling did weaving in the room at the side of the house. It was called Abbots Weave and she used to send the cloth to Scotland to be teased up. Miss Jobling was also area organiser for Home Helps. They owned the adjoining orchard, which they sold to Mr and Mrs Crisp. The couple both died in 1964 aged 86 and 92 and Major Spencer and Mrs. Georgina Murphy purchased the house in the same year. Affectionately always known as Spud and Georgie, they arrived with their teenage children, Nick and Jane. Sadly Jane died in 2000, less than 2 years after her father.

The Murphy's bought back the orchard next door, which had been a market garden and then resold it as a building plot in 1973 after a release of restrictive covenant on the land.

Spencer had remained with the army until he retired and they both took an active part in village life. Georgie was devoted to the church being Secretary for many years and an expert flower arranger. In 2003 she moved to Scotland to be near her son but returned to Isle Abbots for her funeral in 2009.

GREGGS

There was a conveyance on this property with a Mr James Grigg in 1813 but the house was probably built much earlier. It was certainly a shop since the first census when the Patten family ran it. There were other lines of Pattens in the village not connected with the shop. 1841 John Patten, then aged 40, was listed as shopkeeper living with wife Honor 34, their children Ann 6, Harriott 4, Ellen 3 and Heman 2. By 1851 John was described as a Baker and shopkeeper. 16-year-old Anna was then a shop assistant.

By 1861 John was without a wife, Anna was listed as housekeeper, Maria (could be Harriott) as shop attendant, Ellen 23 a dressmaker, Heman, 22, a baker, Luke 18. a Baker's assistant and Laura 15.

The name Post Office and shop appears in 1871, Luke the apprentice was now the baker and Heman a farm bailiff. John was 80 by 1881 and assisted by just his single daughters Ann and Ellen.

The shop continued to be run by the sisters but by 1911 Anna and Ellen are listed as retired shopkeepers. The property was advertised as a shop and post office and sold at auction in 1931 when it was purchased by Harry Priddle who lived there with his first wife Ellen who sadly died in 1937 aged 49 under very unusual circumstances. A doctor and nurse were present at the house when Mrs Priddle was to have 12 teeth extracted by a dental surgeon. The cause of death was given as 'nervous shock and general anaesthesia resulting in cardiac failure.'

Mr Priddle then married Violet Habberfield and they lived in Greggs with their daughter Sheila.

Harry was born in Hambridge and came to Isle Abbots to work as a carpenter at Tapps (Colliers) repairing wagons. He became self-employed mending wagons and making wheelbarrows. Vi kept the accounts. He owned the orchard opposite Greggs and made coffins in the barns, mended wagons, and made wheelbarrows along with doing small carpentry jobs. Vi used to line the coffins and make pillows to go under the head and each side of the face. The material was thick and white with embossed flowers bought from Smiths the undertakers. The coffins were made from Elm or Oak. The last funeral that Harry did cost £32 for an oak coffin, 4 bearers, digging and making up the grave.

Harry also owned land where Willersley and the 4 council houses stand and where the poultry houses are. At one time they kept a Guernsey cow that Harry milked with Vi making the cream. Mr and Mrs. Causton, who lived at Monks Thatch loved the cream and often sent their housekeeper Rhodda to collect it.

The next residents were William (Treg.) and Eve Treganowan who lived there until they had both died and the house was sold again in 1995 to the present owner.

ELM CLOSE

Bill Clarke built this bungalow for Harry and Violet Priddle who moved there in 1973 from Greggs across the road. Their daughter Sheila attended the village school and was taught by Miss Hutchings and Miss Dibble, before attending Ilminster Grammar School. Vi was an active member of the church and at one time Churchwarden. After Harry died Vi continued to live there until she had to go into care when the bungalow was sold and the new owners extended the property. It changed hands again in 2009, the same year that she died.

Bill Clarke building the wall for Elm Close

THE OLD BAKEHOUSE

The first mention of a baker on these premises as being separate from the shop next door is in 1881 when James Lee and his wife Cornelia lived there with James' 13-year-old brother listed as a baker's apprentice. By 1891 the bakery was run by George Hayman, his wife Bessie and 4 young children. This may be the same Hayman family who owned a bakery in Ilton until the late 20th

Century with a shop in Ilminster. By 1901 the cottage was just a house belonging to William Clarke a groom, his wife Annie and infant son William, who were still there by 1911. The infant William, known as Bill, lived in the village for the rest of his life and became a builder. He built a new bungalow in the village called Abbots Glen and finished his days in Glenfields, where his wife Gertrude remained living until moving to Hampshire to be with family. The Clarke's rented out The Bakehouse to Charlie and Lily Mear for many years and when Lily died the cottage was sold and has changed hands several times. Bill and Gertrude were great supporters of the Chapel and even when Bill was quite elderly he could be seen cutting the hedge and weeding the road edge outside the chapel.

TALATA

Bill Clark who had been brought up next door (in the Bakehouse) extended the rear of this old cottage in approximately 1930. As well as using the workshops at the rear for his building business he had a sideline of cutting hair there as well! For some time the cottage was lived in by Ralph and Elizabeth Bicknell. He was always known as 'Bick' and died in the late 1970s. Bick enjoyed making rocking horses in his workshop during his retirement. Elizabeth spent many happy hours researching the history of Isle Abbots and writing the first book about the village. She also collected newspaper cuttings, photos, house sales particulars and many items that have been of enormous help in writing this book and keeping alive snippets of the past that would otherwise have been lost and we owe a great debt to her. Elizabeth died in 1999 aged 88 and the house was sold to the present owners.

2 CHURCH STREET

Due to the uncertain nature of the order of the census, the first clear listing is in 1871 when George Marsh, a Veterinary Surgeon and Castrator lived there with his wife and 16-year-old son as assistant vet. 1901 shows Mr Mark Adams, agricultural labourer, wife Mary and sons John, a carter and Albert, a ploughboy.

Albert Adams lived in this cottage nearly all his life. He moved there age 9 with his parents Mr and Mrs Mark Adams having lived elsewhere in the village for 18 months before. Albert married Nellie (nee Crocker) and they lived with his parents. They celebrated their Diamond Wedding anniversary in 1973. They were affectionately known to everyone in the village as "Uncle Albert and Auntie Nellie", although they had no children of their own. Albert started work at Bromes Farm when he was 11. His wage was 2/6d a week plus a quart of milk each day. By the time he married it had risen to 13/-. Their names were synonymous with the Chapel, as Albert was a local preacher for many years and became senior Deacon of the Baptist Church and Nellie was caretaker at the Chapel for over 50 years.

Albert retired in 1958 after an accident at the milking unit at Badbury when a cow kicked him.

Elizabeth Bicknell

'Bick' with his Jack Russell

Auntie Nellie and Uncle Albert Adams of 2 Church Street, celebrating their golden wedding, 1962

The couple kept ducks in the stone shed opposite the house and it is still known as the 'Duck House'. Albert aged 89 and Nellie aged 85 died within 6 days of each other in 1974.

The cottage was sold in 1975 for £5,225 and has had several owners since.

BOWEYS CORNER / HOMESTILL

This refers to the junction outside what is now Homestill No 1 Church Street. For many years the Bowey family lived there and it is still known locally by that name.

The first mention of a Bowey in Isle Abbots was when William Bowey was a servant aged 12 at Two Bridges Farm in 1861. However, ten years later a William Bowey, possibly the same man, was mentioned at 1 Church Street. He is listed as an agricultural labourer living with wife Prudence and Thomas aged 4, and nephew Ephraim. By 1881 his son, then aged 14 had become a ploughboy and the nephew had been replaced with another lodger, Mary Ann Winter, his sister-in-law, and the house had been listed as being called Edmonds.

"Bowey's Corner" 1907, 1 Church Street and Laurel Cottage behind

By 1891 his wife Elizabeth was 28, so maybe this was a second wife. A stepdaughter was 7 and his children aged 7, 4, 2 and 7 months, along with his mother aged 71 described as a pauper. By 1911 only the mother, a widow with 4 children and a lodger remained.

Olive born about 1900 was the second youngest Bowey child born at Homestill. In 2001 her daughter Barbara Painter (nee Windmill) from the USA visited Barbara Rickitt in Isle Abbots to see where her mother had grown up. Olive had been living in Pinner when she died but her daughter had managed to make a tape of her recalling her childhood days in Isle Abbots. Olive said that after her father died the local families were good to them and what a happy childhood it was. She even remembered the disastrous wedding in 1907 when the vicar read out the burial service by mistake. She remembers that the church was in a ruinous state when it was restored about 1909 and how her brother had found the Roman coffin (the sarcophagus now in the church), during the restoration work and cleaned it up. The family were members of the Baptist Chapel and she went to the village school. She could remember the old orchards and the names of the cider apples. Olive had special permission to leave school at 13 to go into service at Hatch Court. The stable boy came to fetch her. They thought she was very small and gave her milk still warm from the Jersey cow to build her up. Her bedroom was next to the clock tower with its churning cogs but she got used to it. The staff attended morning prayers at 9am. At 13 her wages were 10/- a month. After 4 years she moved to a job in London looking after children.

Another local family moved into Homestill in 1942. Frances Derrick along with her parents and Gran. moved from Abbots Cottage. Her older siblings had left home by then. On leaving the village school Frances cycled to work at Hobbs the Drapers at the bottom of New Road, Ilminster. Then during the war she was moved to Standard Telephone and Cables, as she was too young to be sent away.

In 1948 Frances married Ted Burgess and moved to Axminster where he was a carpenter. But after her father died they both moved into Homestill with her mother and Gran.

The whole family had been brought up as members of the Chapel and her mother was frowned upon for attending the Church's Mothers Union. Frances played the Chapel Organ for many years up until the time it closed. Ted died in 1999 and after the house was sold Frances moved into a flat in Ilminster but continued her interest in the village especially helping with reminiscences of her early life and school days. She remembered all the Chapel outings and Sunday school parties and prize giving when books were given for good attendance. She recalled going to Bromes Farmhouse to collect milk and beautiful clotted cream. They would go around the back of the house and wait in the lean-to by the kitchen. Frances died on 31st January 2016 and sadly did not see this finished book, which she contributed much to.

Frances Burgess

~~~ Education: Schools and the Playgroup ~~~

THE FIRST SCHOOL

On 25th September 1854 an act was enrolled to donate a parcel of land as a school in Isle Abbots. James Atterton Ilott of Glastonbury, whose family had connections with the village, gave the land. It was a piece of ground not exceeding a quarter of an acre being the northern part of the close of land 254 on the tithe map. The one-roomed building was constructed 'For the education of children and adults or children only of the labouring, manufacturing and other poor classes under the control of the Minister and Churchwardens.' The building still exists today, largely unchanged externally as the **Isle Abbots Jubilee Room.**

There are no known records of how many children or adults attended. There was a fireplace for heat, and presumably there must have been an outside toilet at one time.

The earliest known picture of pupils at the Board School

In the 1851 census Alice Burrows was recorded as a schoolmistress and it is believed she taught in the village although the Committee of Council did not certify her. Mr & Mrs Burrows and their seven children lived at the Vicarage, which was rented out at the time.

THE BOARD SCHOOL

The earliest Admission Register for the Board School dates from the day it opened on 7th January 1878. Two other books contain the School Log and the Sales Book date from 1910 until 1959. These are held at the Somerset Records office. The Log Book shows the inspectors' records and the Mistresses' comments on the children's progress and attendance. Children from Isle Brewers also attended the school, but from the registers it looks like they did not start attending in any number until 1919.

The first recorded teacher on 7th January 1878 was Ellen Allen but she only stayed until 1st November. During the first year 67 children were admitted to the school, although some left during the year as they moved away from the parish.

On 6th January 1879, Laura Hewlett was appointed, and recorded in 1881 as living in the attached schoolhouse along with her twelve year old servant Jane Chorley. Then followed Eliza Comley for just 9 months in 1882; Cordelia Bowman from October 1882 until June 1885 and Alice Looman from June 1885 until February 1889.

Remarks in the registers indicated that many of the girls left to go into service or to help their mothers when around twelve years old. Boys also left to go to work around this age, mainly on the farms. Others were noted for non-attendance.

Pupils at the Board school - date unknown

Poor little Fanny Mear and Alexander Hooper appeared to be only just 3 years old when they started school. David Vile who started school at 4 years old left after 2 months, as he was 'too young to come alone'. The Tapp family children often left to be taught privately, and in the case of George the remarks said 'gone to better class school'!

In 1888 both Helen and William Grabham from Ashford left to attend Ilminster Grammar School. Gradually the numbers leaving to attend the Grammar school increased.

By 1891 the schoolhouse was occupied by a widowed retired schoolmistress from Langport, Rhoda Newberry, along with her 21-year-old daughter Matilda Newberry who was the schoolmistress from February 1889 until September 1895.

In 1900 Beatrice Priest left because she was over 12 and her sister Phyllis left in 1901 because she was over 13. It would appear that by about 1910, 14 years old was the leaving age.

Illnesses included measles, ringworm and dirty heads. Children were also absent while helping their parents at home. The autumn floods prevented the Isle Brewers children from attendance, as did heavy snow in February and March 1915 and 1917. An outbreak of Measles and Whooping Cough was recorded in 1912 and again in 1917.

In January 1896 Clara Helena Martindale was appointed as the new Head teacher. She was a qualified teacher and had also received certificates in freehand, model & perspective drawing and another for blackboard drawing. Her annual salary in 1901 was £55. Her husband Albert, who was described as pupil teacher, only received a salary of £5 per year, with a bonus of 5 guineas if the Government Report was satisfactory! Mrs Martindale taught until 1924, but there is no record of when Mr Martindale left. He was not a popular man in the village but Mrs Martindale was a good teacher and a kindly person. They had one daughter, Gladys.

The school summer holidays were called the harvesting holiday, but children often also took time off to help their parents on the farms. In one September during the 1914-18 war two and a half days of Blackberrying by the children produced 70lbs of berries.

1909 school photograph outside the Baptist Chapel
Albert Martindale (centre back row), husband of Headmistress Clara Martindale
Olive Bowley, 2nd from the right lived at Homestill

Other items noted in the logbook 1910 to 1959
1910
- 44 pupils; girls attended cookery lessons in Ilton
- *23rd September*: The school was closed for one week to enable children to pick blackberries. The Head Teacher reported that many children stayed away longer.
- Noel Schofield and Benjamin Bicknell won scholarships to Ilminster Boys' Grammar School.
- Floods prevented children from attending.

1911
- *24th April.* Lucy Chorley commenced to teach the infants as monitor.
- *16th June.* School closed for one week for Coronation
- *31st August.* Harvest Holiday – 3 weeks.
- *September.* Blackberry picking – 1 week.
- *14th September.* No school this afternoon as so many children were going to be absent. A large fete will be held about three miles away.

1912
- Inspector's Report – generally good. However, he did comment 'The children read, recite and speak in a monotonous and indistinct manner.' (Inspectors would report on general organisation, speech training, compositional exercises, drawing, arithmetic, singing, needlework and scripture).

1913
- *29th May.* No school this afternoon as nearly all children went to Club Festival at Fivehead.
- *29th August.* Ringworm reported.

1914
- *13th March.* High flood.
- Inspector reported that 'Infants class was taught by a monitor not yet 15 years of age.' School doing well. However, he stated 'Backs should be provided to seats, at least for younger scholars in main room.' It was not unknown for older scholars (9/10 years) to be placed in class with infants.
- *August* – Boys absent to help with harvest

In the period 1910 to 1916, the average attendance dropped from 40 to 26 pupils

1916
- Measles outbreak

1917
- *27th March.* Mrs Allan visited school and brought a small garment made by the Queen.
- Heating problem lasted several months. Cookery classes at Curry Mallet.
- *22nd June.* Children generally tired and listless. It seems difficult to raise them. They do not go to bed early enough.

1918
- *14th January.* Heavy fall of snow, so no school.

1921
- *11th November.* Today was the anniversary of the Signing of the Armistice (1918) and the children sold poppies. A service was held in church.

1923
- The inspector commented 'The Headmistress has been in charge of the school for 26 years. Though approaching the end of her service, her control is still successful.'
- Suggestion made to establish a library.

1924
- *12th December.* Knitting mentioned.
- *19th December.* Clara Martindale retired and Alyce Hutchings appointed as Headmistress and Miss Chorley as Supplementary teacher.

1925
- *8th June.* Scarlet Fever
- *22nd June.* Whooping cough
- *27th November.* Children attended Memorial Service at St Mary's Church for late Queen Alexandra.

1926
- School role 33 pupils
- *31st August.* New Cloakrooms
- Dental treatment for pupils

1930
- School role 45 pupils
- Regular references made to pupils, particularly from Isle Brewers and Braden areas not being able to attend school because of flooding.
- Marjorie and Sylvia Habberfield admitted to Ilminster Grammar School.

1931
- Curriculum extended to include History and PT. Bernard Habberfield joined school in November.

1932
- Children entered Chard & District Sports, held in Ilminster. School visits to Windsor Castle and Bristol Zoo

1936
- Scarlet Fever.

1937
- Three extra days holiday to celebrate Coronation of King George VI and Queen Elizabeth.

1939
- *1st September.* 'Notice received this morning that school is to be closed during evacuation.
- *11th September.* School re-opened. No mention of extra evacuee children.

It does seem strange that no comments were made in the school logbook about the evacuee children who attended school, although their names and addresses were recorded in the registers. An article from the Daily Mirror on 31st August 1944 mentions 'Overcrowded Ile Abbots has one real problem, though, "What is going to happen when the children start school?" they ask. The village schoolroom is just big enough to accommodate the twenty three regulars, but with seventeen other pupils the little room belonging to the Baptist Chapel may have to be brought into use.'

1932

Back Row: Kenneth Brice, Edwin Goodland, Leslie Slade, Edwin Chorley, Alex Welsher, Bill Harvey, Ronald Earley
Second Row: Winnie Adams, Irene Bennett, Mary Derrick, Audrey Brice, Marjorie Habberfield, Dorothy Burton, Vera Burton, Elsie Davey
Third Row: Douglas Earley, Gordon Priddle, Cyril Drake, ? Burton, Dennis Brice
Fourth Row: Sylvia Habberfield, Clive Bennett, Jim Watts, Sydney Derrick, Eric Goodland, Charlie Dare
Sitting: Eva Goodland, Dorothy Davey, Ronald Adams, Bernard Habberfield, Ronald Mead, Kathleen Derrick, Frances Derrick
Teachers: Miss Alice Hutchings   Miss Hilda Osborne

1945
- *8th May.* School closed for two days to celebrate the end of war in Europe.
- *5th September.* Two extra days holiday for VJ day.

1948
- *5th January.* School role only 21.
- *21st March.* Silver Wedding Anniversary of King George VI and Queen Elizabeth.

1954
- Reference to school bus not being able to get through floods.
- *21st July.* Open afternoon for parents and friends to see work of school.
- Collection taken towards cost of wireless set.

SCHOOL SPORTS DAY c.1950

Reverend Probert is seated in the middle of the ladies with Mrs Probert on his right. Miss Salmon, from Badbury, sporting the hat with flowers Violet Priddle with daughter Sheila on her lap. Winnie Burgess with Heather and Richard on lap. Margaret Squires and Gwen Dare (two of the young girls). Also present: Miss Chorley, Miss Dibble, Mrs Bristow, Mrs Hobbs..

1955
- *19th December.* Concert this evening for parents and friends.

1956
- *16th April.* Clerical assistant appointed.
- *29th May.* Fire drill.
- *26th September.* School closed for Bridgwater Fair.
- *18th December.* Concert

1958
- Only 13 children attend school, polio inoculations.

THE SCHOOL CLOSED ON MARCH 20th. 1959.

The school building has since become the village hall and the house is now in private ownership.

Isle Abbots School Closure

Last Friday was a sad day for Ile Abbots as the school was officially closed as from that day. The teacher, Miss L.C.Grandorge has been at the school since 1954 and in that time has made herself greatly loved and respected by pupils and parents alike. Miss Grandorge is not likely to leave the village immediately however, as she is to become a supply teacher in the county. Presentations were made to Miss Grandorge and also to Miss Hobbs and Donald Tapp (cleaners). The Vicar, the Rev. D.F.W.Probert, chairman of the School Managers, addressed those assembled for the presentations. Mrs Dare of Two Bridges Farm who made the presentation voiced the feelings of all present in expressing deep regret at the closure of the school and emphasizing the affection and esteem in which Miss Grandorge was held after five years in the village. Miss Grandorge received a clock suitably inscribed; Mrs Hobbs a tea service; and Mr Tapp a cigarette case. The gifts were made possible by subscriptions from pupils, parents and friends of Ile Abbots and Ile Brewers.

1935 younger children

Back Row: Ron Mead, Richard Jefferey, Eileen Davey, Eva Mead, Iris Bennett Betty Mear, Betty Adams
Middle: Ron Adams, Philip Jeffrey, Jim Watts, Eva Goodland, Dennis Brice, Fred Burgess, Bernard Habberfield, Charlie Dare
Sitting: Jim Burgess, Eric Mead, Phyllis Adams, Myra Davey, Norah Adams, Betty Wilsher, Frances Derrick

1935 older children

Back Row: Sid Derrick, Eric Goodland, Cyril Drake, Les Philips, Clive Bennet
Middle: Bill Harvey, Ron Early, Vera Bennet, Audrey Brice, Irene Bennet, Edwin Chorley, Ken Brice.
Sitting: Doris Adams, Dorothy Davey, Majorie Akers, Lily Meakins, Kathleen Derrick, Molly Dare, Sylvia Habberfield

MEMORIES OF SCHOOL DAYS

From a report given by EMILY WINTER (nee Taylor) in 1977, and recorded by her daughter Betty Sheale.

EMILY WINTER hated her school days (1901-1911) She dreaded being late and getting a 'black mark' in the register. It was sometimes unavoidable, as on many mornings she would be sent to her granny's house in Fivehead where she would collect some bread for breakfast. The flooded fields were a nightmare to her after heavy rain as she had a fear of water. She could not refuse to go. The eldest daughter she was expected to run errands.

In Emily's time at school the girls always wore white pinafores over their dresses and their hair, when it was long, was plaited and tied with a ribbon. Naughty boys sitting in desks behind them would dip the ends of the girls' hair in the inkwells.

Emily was always proud that she could read and write. She shone at spelling, very often gaining '10 on 10' for a spelling test. She hated arithmetic. Caroline (her mother) kept Emily's School Leaving Certificate for many years until it disappeared – probably in one of the moves to Tysons, Wellings or Church Cottage, Curry Mallet.

In 1911 Emily lived with her parents Caroline and Henry and 7 brothers and sisters at Lombards.

JACK ADAMS (recorded 1996) remembered the teachers Mr. and Mrs. Martindale as being very strict. Annie Dyte from the village cleaned the school and lit the big boiler. The children were divided into 3 groups.

JOHN HUMPHRY of Woodlands Farm (recorded 1999) started school in 1928 and remembered that he used to go to school early some days and take a jug to fetch the school milk from Bromes Farmhouse. Later he and brother Edward went to Ilminster Grammar School as paying pupils and were weekly boarders with the Headmaster.

BRENDA INNES (nee Adams) (recorded 1999) attended the school until the age of 11. She carved her initials on the school wall and they are still there. The older girls went to Creech St Michael for cookery classes every Friday with Miss Dibble and Miss Hutchens. They shopped at Creech shop and shared the expenses and brought home what they cooked, if it survived the bus ride. When she started in 1941 they still used chalk and a slate. Brenda was left-handed but was forced to write with the right hand, which caused her difficulties.

She remembered going to Bromes Farm to collect the school milk from Miss Hodge, Mr Bicknell's housekeeper who did all the dairy work. There was a ledge by the front gate to rest the milk on and one day she spilt it. It was boiled at the school before they drank it.

One day they had a pantomime at the school, Snow White. She was the youngest and was Dopey. Mr Bushel held practices in Stills Farmhouse.

She remembered air-raid practices during the war. The school children and people in that area had to meet under the large tree by the pond in Waldronds field. They had to take a cushion or blanket to be comfortable during a raid.

FRANCES BURGESS (nee Derrick) (recorded 1999) attended the village school from 1931 to 1940. She remembered school outings to London and going on the river. Also visiting Huntley and Palmers biscuit factory at Reading.

THE PLAYGROUP

Susan Vickery in the garden at Lower Woodlands

Susan Vickery started the playgroup in 1981 at her house Lower Woodlands. With her own growing family and the children of friends in the village, it became a time for the children to play and the parents to get together.

When the playgroup expanded it moved to regular sessions in the village hall with the help of some of the mothers. As rules and regulations became more onerous, leaders had to be qualified and various people have been employed.

Mrs. Christine Blake was the leader from 1999 together with a paid assistant. Children attended from outside the village and the group conformed to all the national curriculum education requirements. When the weather allowed, happy voices could be heard in the playground behind the village hall and they enjoyed occasional walks through the village and sometimes went on outings.

The number of children attending dwindled over the years, and despite fund raising events such as goat racing, fêtes and the very popular Santa Special trains to visit Santa in his grotto at Bromes House, the playgroup finally closed in July 2016.

The Playgroup display at the Queen's Golden Jubilee exhibition 2002. Oliver Lucas, Ross and Ella Colenso

Playgroup fund raising steam-up 2009

Emma visits Santa with Rory and Elise, December 2015

~~~ Isle Abbots in the two World Wars ~~~

WORLD WAR 1 1914-1918

There were 31 men and one lady, Alice Kelly a V.A.D. nurse, who ventured forth, probably full of enthusiasm to serve their country and see the world. They must have found life very different from sleepy Isle Abbots and the farms would have been affected from lack of workers.

The following list is of parishioners who served in the 1914-18 war, some of whom were already in the Regular Army.

Allan, H.S., 2nd Liet., 6th London Regt. India & France
Bicknell, J.M., pte. France
Bicknell, T.F.W., pte. France
Crocker. Pte. Home Service
Chorley, H.J., sergt. France
Chorley, W.T., pte., W.S.Y., Gallipoli, Egypt, Palestine, France
Cuff, C.R., H.M.S. Australia
Dare, C.H., France
Davey, C. gunner. France
Davey, J., pte. France
Davis, S., pte. France
Grigg, H., gunner. R.M.A., with siege guns in France
Hembrow, H.M.S. Lion
Hooper, W.C., pte. Home Service
Hooper. Pte. France
Hooper, A., pte. France
Hooper, J., pte. France
Hooper, W.J., pte. France
Hull, A.W., pte. Gallipoli, Egypt, France
Hull, W.J.O., pte. France
Humphry, J.H., corp. S.W.Y., Gallipoli, Egypt, Palestine, France
Kelly, Alice. Nurse, V.A.D., France and Home Service
Mear. Pte. France
Mear, S.F., pte. France
Payne, H.J., driver, France
Poundsbury, C., pte. R.G.A., France
Poundsbury, P., A.S.C.M.T., France
Poundsbury, W.S., corp. Sc. Rifles, France and Salonika
Tapp, W.J., sergt. major. R.A.M.C., France
Taylor, F.J., pte. France
Taylor, E.J., pte. France
Taylor, H.C., driver, France

There are photos of those who served in the church. The original photos, which hung in the vestry, had deteriorated and have been digitally repaired and reproduced. Some of the identities were not clear but were confirmed as far as possible by older members of the village.

One young man was Driver Henry Charles Taylor known to his family as 'Char'. He was the eldest child of Henry Charles Taylor & Caroline (nee Edmonds) of Lombards. He was awarded the 1914-15 Star, the British War Medal and the Victory Medal. His niece Betty Sheale thinks that the vicar gave everyone who went to war a cloth covered bible.

Driver Henry Charles Taylor

The inscription inside 'Char's' read ....

1914 To Driver Henry Charles Taylor, No 17213, C. Sub-Section
B. Battery, 109th Brigade 24th Division, R J.A. On Active Service
    from his affectionate Mother Caroline Taylor,
        Lombards House, Isle Abbots, nr. Taunton, Somerset, England
    'The Eternal God is thy refuge; and He shall thrust out
    the enemy from before thee and shall say, "Destroy them!"
    Deuteronomy 33c 27v
    'Fear thou not, for I am with thee
    Rev Gibbons Isaiah 41c 10v

The village collected £64.2s.11d. for a brass memorial plaque on the church wall commemorating those who gave their lives between 1914-1919. It reads ...

"To the glory of God and in grateful and affectionate memory of those of this parish who gave their lives in the Great War. This tablet is erected by parishioners & friends".
Rev. Henry Somerset Allan, 2nd Lieut:6th London Regt: (India & France) John Mansfield Bicknell, West Som: Yeomanry (Sigr:France) Charles Davey, Gunner R.G.A. (France) William John Hooper, Pte. P.A.S.L.I. (France).

There are no minutes in the Parish Council Minute Book for the war years.

In a conversation with Jack Adams in 1996 he remembered when war broke out. He was 7 at the time. At the end of the war sports were held in the field behind the present bus shelter. He remembered Edward Davey being naughty and the teacher shut him in the school as punishment, but he climbed out of a window and joined in the sports anyway. A celebratory tea was held in barns at Manor Farm as it was raining.

WORLD WAR 2 1939-1945

There is more evidence of life in the village during the Second World War as this has been recorded from living memory and written records. The bright yellow tractors in the village were painted green to camouflage them. The signpost at Roundoak was taken down and the village name erased from the school.

More land was ploughed for the food effort. The greatest impact was made by the purchase of land at Woodlands by the Air Ministry. The site was named Merryfield after Sir Nicholas Wadham's old mansion nearby. American airmen arrived there in 1944 and used it for most of that year flying Dakotas to the D Day landings. A hospital unit was established for their casualties. Each month saw the comings and goings of different flights and squadrons taking troops abroad. After the Dakotas came Halifax's and Liberators. Towards the end of 1944 the station was transferred to the R.A.F. and closed down in 1946. The airfield was reopened in 1972 and is now used to train helicopter pilots for the Royal Navy.

According to school records a notice was received on 1st September 1939 to say it was to close during evacuation. It then re-opened on 11th September. The room at the back of the chapel was used as an extra schoolroom.

The Daily Mirror article dated August 31, 1944 tells of evacuees in the village.

WARTIME MEMORIES

When the airfield was being built Phyllis Tapp (nee Derrick) recalled how she worked in the canteen feeding workers, many of them were rough Irishmen. She remembered the first American planes coming in bringing tanks, supplies and of course the Americans. After this she was drafted to Tone Vale Mental Hospital as a live in domestic.

Jack Adams remembered when Americans were stationed at Merryfield Airfield between Isle Abbots and Ilton and this brought a bit of extra interest to the village. He remembers when the Americans went to Curry Mallet Pub by bike or walking across the fields coming out by Curry Mallet church. One night one of them threw a bike over the hedge of Tysons, stamped RAF, and it was never reclaimed.

Jack also remembered when 3 Germans bailed out of a plane over Golden Hill. Two of them knocked at the dairy at Bradon and the dairy lady took them to Mrs

Tiny village sets a big example in country's duty

39 FIND REFUGE IN ITS 44 HOUSES

By Your Special Correspondent

TUCKED away somewhere in a crazy pattern of twisting roads, the sleepy village of Ile Abbots, Somerset, has every reason to overlook the war.

In its isolation it has not been changed by buzz-bombs or the old-fashioned ones. Its apples and cherries grow in profusion. Its dogs sleep in the roadway. Life goes on, as it has always gone on, slowly and leisurely.

But the 140 people of Ile Abbots have put themselves in the war. They have taken thirty-nine evacuees from London and Southern England, and housed them in most of their forty-four picturesque, thatch-roofed cottages.

Somerset is proud of Ile Abbots, the tiny village that has done a big job of work. But Ile Abbots is surprised at the fuss that is being made of it.

"Evacuees are nothing new to us," says Mrs. Priddle, wife of the village carpenter. "They came during the 1940 blitzes in London, and we've had them off and on ever since.

"This time they're a bit more than usual. We've nearly all taken somebody, but look at all the evacuees that people have taken in all over the country."

Seventeen children and twenty-two elderly people have in five weeks become part and parcel of the village. The church of St. Mary has a bigger congregation than ever and the queue at the bus stop, a mile up one of the twisting roads, is longer than it has ever been for the two buses that run every day into Taunton.

School Problem

Overcrowded Ile Abbots has one real problem, though. "What is going to happen when the children start school?" they ask.

The village schoolroom is just big enough to accommodate the twenty-three "regulars," but with seventeen other pupils the little room belonging to the Baptist Chapel may have to be brought into use.

Said Mrs. Causton, the village WVS chief: "The children are enjoying themselves and are beginning to look healthier and stronger.

"Some of them help on the farms where they are billeted, but most of them spend their days playing in the lanes and searching the hedges for blackberries.

"We've been expecting to have to telephone Nurse Clarke some time, but there's been no need so far."

Some of the evacuee children in Church-street, Ile Abbots, near Taunton, Somerset, waiting for the village postman to arrive. This tiny picturesque village of forty-four cottages has thirty-nine evacuees from London and Southern England—seventeen children and twenty-two elderly people.

The Daily Mirror of August 31st 1944 carried the story of the 39 evacuees who came to Isle Abbots to escape the bombing of Southern England.

Goodland at Ashford who gave them a cup of tea. They were taken away as prisoners of war. The third man's parachute did not open and sometime later a farmer on horseback in a field had his horse keep snorting and refusing to go on, he got off to look and found the body in a ditch.

Jack worked for the Ilminster milk factory and one day when he was driving his lorry with milk to Somerton Milk Factory it was bombed and 11 people were killed, so he was sent on to Wincanton.

During the war he took his turn at patrolling the village at night. He had to collect his ARP whistle from Greggs Cottage.

Jack and his wife Sis had 2 evacuees at Tysons and later in their council house that had just been built in Manor Road. The boys Peter and Rodney grew fond of them and kept in touch.

Brenda Innes also remembered the Americans at Merryfield. She would go with her sister to visit them and they gave them custard creams. At the end of the war the Americans gave a party for local children and they had to take their own mug, plate and cutlery.

Dick Lucas of Higher Woodlands, who at the time worked on the family farm in Puckington, was in the Home Guard that was based at Woodhouse by the airfield. He remembered the airmen going out with local girls and the Dakotas at Merryfield and how they went off to D Day towing 2 gliders behind full of troops.

John Humphry also worked on the family farm at Woodlands and was in the Home Guard. During the war 100 acres of farmland was compulsory purchased for the airfield. There was an old farm workers cottage on this land, which was used to store land mines. After the war it was decided these were too dangerous to move and the cottage was blown up one hot Saturday morning in August. Everyone in the vicinity was evacuated and they had to leave all the doors and drawers in his house at Woodlands Farm open to save any damage. John and his family went to the top of Rock Hill and watched the explosion. It made a lot of dust in the house but nothing was broken. A field of wheat surrounding the house was absolutely flattened.

John also remembered another 20-acre smallholding and house that was demolished to make room for the airfield. This cottage was known as the Saltbox but he could not remember its proper name.

Edmund Dare who as a child was living in a cottage at Roundoak (since demolished), can remember there being a gun in the garden and that on Christmas Day the Yanks at the airfield put up loud speakers with Christmas Carols and lights. He also remembered that a flag pole was tied to a pinnacle on the church tower to celebrate VE Day.

Peter Jacobson who at the time of writing is nearly 90 and living in Australia, recalls vividly when he moved to the village from Croydon with his family for safety during the war. He was sent to Taunton School and his sister to Weirfield School in Taunton.

"……..It was lovely in Isle Abbots harvesting and making cider at the Habberfields. I joined the ATC flight being formed in Fivehead. I was a year under age but they needed one more to provide the minimum 15 cadets!

"It was 1942 and an opportunity arose for a seven-day experience at a wartime training aerodrome plus a promise of a flight in an aircraft. We went by RAF Regiment lorries from Fivehead to Westonzoyland. I took my bike and Wellington boots and a 'gas cape' as rain was forecast. It sure did, it poured the whole seven days and we were under canvas and unable to do much but attend lectures. All planes were grounded.

"Two of us decided to stay on as it wasn't raining on the Sunday. We both had flights in a Boulton Paul Defiant. We then rode home, David to Langport and myself to Isle Abbots. It was latish but now a cloudless night with a bright near full moon lit up the whole area and coming down the hill from Fivehead all I could see was a sea of water. When I reached the waters edge it was obvious I could not cycle the road into the village, but Bill, one of Mr. Habberfield's farm hands lived on a rise close by. So I went to his house and left my bike there. Bill was a fine dairyman and he had his own dog Bob. I knew of the footbridge across the field from his house and the stile that led into the village. Bill said it was shallow enough, the river was dropping but it flowed fast and I would have to keep a firm grip on the one rail and watch my footing on the narrow plank. Bill supplied me with a stave to test the depth of the waters. I had not noticed Bob but he ran ahead and insisted on leading me across right to the stile. I was only fourteen and a half at the time."

~~~~ Shopping ~~~~

William Humphry was shown in the 1841 census as being an Innkeeper. So liquid refreshment for the many farm labourers would have been obtained from there. By 1861 the Inn had closed and William was listed as a farmer. His daughter Hannah was a shopkeeper in 1871 but it is not clear where.

It has always been known that Waldron was the butcher. There are many Waldrons mentioned in the church registers from 1734. But an entry in 1765 says that Jane daughter of William Waldron (Butcher) and his wife Martha was baptised. So the family were certainly butchers from that time on, if not before. Whether they sold their meat on the premises or delivered it is not clear.

Delivery boy in Church Street - from a postcard postmarked 1908

The BAKERY was in the main street where a cottage known as the Old Bakery stands.

The house next door called Greggs was a post office and shop, certainly from the mid 1800s run by John Patten. His two daughters Ellen and Anna assisted him in later life. His son, Heman, was listed as being a Bakers Boy aged 11 in 1851.

A 1931 sales catalogue for the estate of Miss Patten describes the house now known as Greggs as "A picturesque cottage and small shop, known as The Old Post Office, built of stone with thatched roof, and very pleasantly situated in Church Road, with sunny aspect, and containing sitting room with grate, living room with open-beamed fireplace, scullery, pantry, small shop (formerly used as the Post Office), lean-to at the side which can be converted into a garage, two bedrooms and a loft. At the rear is a large garden with lean-to and well of water. On the opposite side of the road a useful stone built and tiled building with stable."

At the same time Tilley's Orchard opposite was also for sale, and Mr. Harry Priddle purchased the whole lot.

There was once a shop at Harvest Cottage, half shop and half cottage lived in by Kate Adams. *Vi Priddle remembered when this shop was also known as Lanes. Miss Lane lived in the Old Manse set back from Harvest Cottage. A Miss Drake also assisted in the shop. Frances Burgess remembered it as a funny little shop with partitions made of Tea chests. It sold all sorts of food items and paraffin.*

Ellen and Ann Patten

- 95 -

Mrs Gray in the shop

Mr. Drake ran the village shop before Mrs. Gray took over the Post Office and Shop in part of the house known now as Monks Cottage. It was a happy meeting place for villagers for over twenty years until she retired in 1974. At a farewell gathering the Parish Council Chairman presented a radio to Mrs. Gray on her retirement as village postmistress and shopkeeper. Jennifer Humphry also presented Mrs. Gray with a bouquet of flowers and the ladies of the village produced light refreshments for all.

Captain and Mrs Gray had built a bungalow at the bottom of the garden for their retirement. This was approached from Blind Lane and called Avalon.

Abbots Nursery run by Mr & Mrs Crisp next to the Post Office

The house and shop was sold and the telephone box and letterbox moved to a different position. Next came Ken and Kate Taylor who for a while ran the post office and sold antiques. Ken was born at Lumbards Cottage; and was grandson of Henry Charles and Caroline Taylor who had many children at Lumbards.

Vi Priddle remembered when Mr. Drake owned this shop and when you paid the bill on a Saturday morning, he gave away a bar of chocolate. Her young brother Bernard Habberfield always appeared on his bike at this time and she gave it to him.

The next owners Grenville and Margaret Massman ran a part time post office as a service to the village. Along with other small post office owners he protested about business rates. A newspaper article in 1990 states "I'm determined to keep the post office going at all costs as a service to the village. At the moment I am protesting against the business rate." Mr. Massman believes that a post office open for just 20 hours a week is operating as a community service, not a business. He said, "From a personal point of view the whole thing is uneconomic in the first place, but I don't mind because I'm prepared to help the OAPs." In addition to the imposition of the business rate post offices are obliged to collect payments of the community charge, for which they receive no fee. Mr. Massman is also angry with the electricity board, which charges a commercial rate for the whole premises. So eventually when Mr. Massman could no longer carry on the village lost its post office and even the telephone box was decommissioned in the early 21st century.

During the 1950s Mrs. Probert the vicars' wife sold National Savings Stamps.

There have been many delivery vans bringing food and services to the village over the years.

John Steele remembered when Harveys' travelling shop used to come to the village, which carried practically everything. It had canvas sides and you could hear it coming, as the paraffin lamps etc. that were hanging on the side would clatter about.

He also remembered Harry Mould the harness maker from North Curry who used to come round in his pony and trap every other week selling and repairing harnesses and other leather goods.

Mr. Pickford from Roundoak grew vegetables and went around selling them from his car on Saturdays. At one time meat was delivered by a Mr. Gould.

Haymans the bakers used to deliver bread until they felt compelled to stop the round in 1974 saying "labour and abnormal overheads all conspire to make the situation uneconomic, at least in small isolated communities."

Harry Mould the Harness Maker

Mr. Gould's Van in Church Street

Mrs. Phyllis Burton who lived at Uttermares Cottages chose to cycle to Ilminster for some of her shopping. When her husband Bill was alive they would grow lots of vegetables in the front garden. In 1989 she had a big surprise for her 80th birthday – see the newspaper article. Phyllis died in January 1991 aged 81.

50 years in the saddle

A MYSTERY turned into a birthday surprise for 80-year-old cyclist Mrs Phyllis Burton.

For 50 years Mrs Burton (pictured above) has cycled into Ilminster twice a week for her shopping, returning to her home at Isle Abbotts with her basket and two carrier bags full of groceries.

Last week when she went shopping she left her bicycle at a friend's house in Court Barton, but as she was preparing to return home, she saw it parked outside a butcher's shop.

Thinking someone may have stolen it, she went to investigate ... only to be 'ambushed' by a group of gift-laden traders.

They presented her with flowers, chocolates, a bottle of drink and a specially made birthday cake for being a loyal customer, and then she was chauffeur-driven home.

From the
CHARD & ILMINSTER NEWS
10th November 1989

Church Street in the days of horse and cart...

for people as well as produce!

~~~ Transport ~~~

Before the age of wheeled transport, footpaths and stiles were well used and people would walk long distances. Then the bicycle became more common. When Francis Derrick left school she was able to cycle to work at Hobbs the drapers at the bottom of New Road in Ilminster. John Steele cycled to his private school in Helland and occasionally went by pony and trap.

Frances Burgess said her uncle Bob ran a horse and cart from Isle Brewers to Taunton on Saturdays. A seat had to be booked in advance by sending a postcard. Phyllis Tapp recalled her late husband Don telling her how there used to be a carriers cart running to Taunton on Saturdays, one from Isle Brewers and one from Fivehead. This was an open cart pulled by horses that his mother used to go on. It was especially busy at Christmas. The horses were rested at an Inn in East Reach, Taunton ready for the return journey.

Charabanc run by E.J. Davis of Ilminster

Harry Humphry from Woodlands Farm was one of the first to have a car in the village. Major John Claude Steele would travel to work in Taunton in a chain driven Trojan car after he retired from the army. Edmund Dare remembers Edgar Habberfield's first car, a canvas topped Vauxhall and Mr. Summers also had a car in 1933/34. Charabanc outings were remembered as an occasional treat, usually to the seaside.

The nearest railway stations to Isle Abbots were at Hatch Beauchamp and Ilton. Hatch (as it was officially called) opened with the Taunton to Chard Railway line in 1866. It had a ticket office, small goods yard and served the farmers in Isle Abbots when such things as teasels and sugar beet were sent elsewhere in the country. At the outset there were six trains in each direction on weekdays.

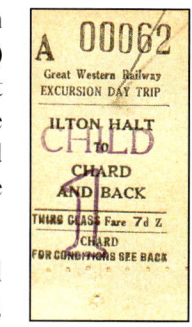

Ilton Halt was a simple structure with a seat and a small shelter and opened in 1928. It was never staffed; passengers bought their tickets from the guard on the train, or at their destination. The platform, however, lives on at a new location at Cranmore East on the East Somerset Railway. Both stations survived until the whole line closed on 10th September 1962.

The village has never been well served by buses. For many years past Southern National - later First Buses have traversed the "top road" between Taunton and Yeovil with a relatively frequent service, but they have never reached Isle Abbots.

Hutchings and Cornelius' brown buses from South Petherton started a service serving the village after the war and by 1961 there were 2 return buses a day from Isle Abbots to Taunton from Monday to Friday, 3 buses each way on Saturday, and no buses on Sundays. By 1978 they only provided a Saturday bus to Taunton.

Hutchings and Cornelius' bus service ended in 1979

In May 1979 the service abruptly ceased and Mrs. Veronica Gunn's red Safeway Service buses, also based at South Petherton, provided a replacement until 2001.

Safeway Services of South Petherton served the village until 2001

In the first decade of the new millennium, Cooks Coaches provided a Thursday service to Ilminster, Berry's Coaches a Wednesday bus to Taunton, and the Somerset County Council minibus went to Taunton on a Saturday morning. At the time of writing the last mentioned is the only surviving service.

The Thursday bus, by then operated by Hatch Green coaches, and supported by Somerset County Council, finally departed on 21st May 2015

The last bus to Ilminster 21st May 2015. The poplar trees have now also gone.

The Huish School bus has been a regular sight in the village for decades. For many years Osmond's Coaches from Curry Rivel provided this service, and then subsequently by Berry's Coaches of Taunton, who are the operators at the time this book was written.

A description in the 1978 Hutchings and Cornelius timetable is rather amusing 'The narrow lanes that turn tail on themselves running through a farmyard or two on their way from village to village lead to places with names as enchanting as their settings. Kingsbury Episcopi, Shepton Beauchamp, Tintinhull, Isle Abbotts, Isle Brewers, Curry Mallet and Curry Rivel sprawl over this lazy landscape where Rivers Isle and Parrett meander aimlessly. The buses meander too, with dizzy irregularity, giving these dotted settlements a reliable service.'

~~~ Special Occasions, Jubilees ~~~

In 1902 the Annual assembly of the Parish Meeting recommended a public meeting to consider the wishes of the parishioners as to a suitable way in which to celebrate the Coronation of King Edward VII and Queen Alexandra.

Again in 1911 a meeting was proposed to consider a suitable way to celebrate the Coronation of His Majesty King George V and Her Majesty Queen Mary. The outcome of both of these occasions is not known.

However, the Silver Jubilee of the reign of King George V was celebrated in great style in May 1935. A local newspaper report quotes…

"This little village looked quite gay and festive with its flags and arches on Jubilee Day and the parish flag floating on the tower.

"A united morning service was held in the church when the vicar Rev. J. F. Alexander officiated and the lesson was read by Mr. T. Derrick. A luncheon was held for the men in the Council School and before sitting down the National Anthem was sung. At the close of the luncheon Mr. J. H. Humphry proposed a toast to the King and all members of the royal family and rousing cheers were given.

"At 4pm the women and children partook of tea. The School was very prettily decorated and Mrs. Akers daintily decorated tables. Afterwards sports were held in a field kindly lent by Mr. E. J. Habberfield. Mrs. Alexander presented money prizes to the winners.

"Mr. J. Humphry presented all the village children with a Jubilee cup, saucer and plate – gifts from H.R.H. the Prince of Wales. Hearty cheers were given to H.R.H. by the school children. This was followed by a most successful social evening, the chief feature of which was a fancy dress parade, which caused laughter and amusement.

All the committees are to be congratulated on the spirit in which they entered into the proceedings and helped to make Jubilee Day something to be remembered".

1937 - School records show that three days extra holiday was given to celebrate the Coronation of King George VI and Queen Elizabeth.

1945 – VE Day 8th May. The School closed for two days to celebrate the end of war in Europe.

1945 – VJ Day 2nd September. Two extra days school holiday were given for VJ Day.

1946 - VICTORY DAY
In May 1946 the Parish Meeting held a special meeting to discuss arrangements for the celebration of Victory Day on June 8th that year. " It was resolved that the children be given a tea and that a United Service be held in the Parish Church. Also, that all parishioners who wished, be taken to Bertram Mills Circus when it next visited Taunton, failing this to the seaside. The money for this to be taken from the fund known as the Isle Abbots Trust." Whether this came to fruition is unknown!

1977 – QUEEN ELIZABETH II SILVER JUBILEE. A street party was held

The 1977 QEII Silver Jubilee Street party

A commemorative horse chestnut tree was planted at Cox's Pit. After many setbacks it has now developed into quite a healthy specimen!

The Silver Jubilee Tree with Fiona Guest, January 1990

1981 – WEDDING OF PRINCE CHARLES & LADY DIANA SPENCER

1995 – 50-Yr. CELEBRATION AFTER VE DAY. A street party was held

The 50-year celebration after VE day, 1995

Jack Adams, Reg Burgess & John Humphry enjoying the VE celebrations 1995

2000 - THE MILLENIUM.

Towards the end of 1999 the Parish Council launched a competition to design a village crest. Sue Gatcombe from Broadfields was the winner. The design suitably depicted the village church, crops growing and a Heron standing in the river. The design has been used on many things since.

- 102 -

With grant money, Derold Page painted a village millennium map. A copy was given to every household, and an extract is inside the front cover.

Martin Rickitt (PC vice-charman) and Derold Page (artist) with the millennium map

New Years Day 2000 was celebrated by a special church service followed by a buffet lunch in the village hall.

2002 – QUEEN ELIZABETH II GOLDEN JUBILEE.

Daisy Parsons, James Cottell, Tom Jay, Tom Sutcliffe, Nellie and George Parsons at the fancy dress parade 3/6/2002

The village really went to town with celebrations of this event. On Saturday 1st June there was a family social evening in the marquee in the grounds of Thimble Hall. Riotous acts were performed by members of the village with little sketches, poems and singing from the Isle Abbots Choir and others.

On Sunday 2nd June a service of Praise in the church was followed by buffet lunch in the village hall. Then in the afternoon sports were held in the grounds of Thimble Hall. On Monday 3rd June, which was dedicated as a National Holiday, there was a fancy dress parade starting at the village hall and walking to a tea party in the main street. Sideshows and a bouncy castle provided entertainment. In the evening a huge bonfire and firework display was held behind Manor Farm with a barbecue.

A small group was formed to put on a display of village history in the Church Room over the weekend. This group also photographed every house in the village, mostly with its occupants standing outside and these were mounted in an album. Members of this group were Barbara Rickitt, David Jay, David Sutcliffe and Peter Cottell.

Peter Cottell, Barbara & Martin Rickitt, David Sutcliffe, David Jay

A grant had been made by Somerset District Council that helped fund these events. The Parish Council had also organised some special mugs to be made, some for sale and some to be given to all the children under the age of 18 in the village.

The Village Choir at Stourhead Gardens, VE Day, 2005

2005 – 60th ANNIVERSARY OF V. E. DAY. In May, the Village Choir, under the leadership of David Sutcliffe, were invited to sing as part of the 'Festival of the Voice at Stourhead Gardens. Choir members dressed in wartime clothes and sang a selection of songs from that era.

2011 – WEDDING OF PRINCE WILLIAM and KATE MIDDLETON.

The village hall committee arranged a street party. Participants provided their own food and arranged to share with neighbours. There was a competition for best-dressed table and fancy dress with a theme of W or K.

David Sutcliffe as Wills at the Royal Wedding street party 2011

George & Daisy Parsons at the Diamond Jubilee Street Party

2012- QUEEN ELIZABETH II DIAMOND JUBILEE

On Sunday 3rd June a special church service was held to mark this momentous occasion, followed by a lunch party in the main street. Friends and neighbours joined forces to share lunch and decorate their tables. The village hall committee arranged a competition for the best 5metre length of bunting, which was erected beforehand, and a 1950 style fancy dress competition. Tea was served outside Church Cottage with cup cakes organised by Daisy Parsons.

On 4th June a Jubilee Beacon was lit by Mervyn Vickery in Woodlands Orchard at 10pm to coincide with the national event, followed by a Barbecue.

On 18th August that year the Village Hall held a Diamond Jubilee themed Ball in the John Steele Memorial Marquee in the grounds of Thimble Hall.

Reggie Colenso

Queen Elizabeth II Diamond Jubilee Street Party
3rd June 2012

~~~ Recreation ~~~

School and chapel outings would have been a real highlight in the village in times gone by. Early outings would have been by Charabanc. Vi Priddle remembered her husband talking about a Charabanc outing to Weymouth and Frances Burgess also remembered chapel outings to Weymouth. Jack Adams recalled a Chapel outing to Teignmouth by Charabanc. It rained all the way and one had to be careful not to touch the canvas roof or the rain came in. Once there, the sun shone and for one old man from the village it was the first time at the seaside.

Both the chapel and church Sunday schools held Christmas parties. Apparently some children worked out that if you attended both for a while you could be invited to two Christmas parties!

The Ladies' Cricket Team
Ethel Gray, Cissie Adams, Lily Mear, Vi Priddle, Mrs Hobbs, Sonia Probert, Lucy Chorley
Middle: Mary Derrick, Winnie Burgess, Front: Brenda Innes, Margaret Squires

At one time the river Isle at Red Bridge was known as the swimming pool. There were steps into the river and a diving board. People would come from some distance away to use this. Frances Burgess was not allowed to swim there, but her family would take picnics along the riverbank towards Bradon, where there was a shallow part with a gravel beach that they could paddle in. Rev. Probert's son Michael learnt to swim in the river Isle and got a Bronze Medal for his swimming.

There was a village cricket team who played behind the orchard at Manor Farm. Brenda Innes used to help with the scoring and sometimes they travelled by bus to other matches. Both Mrs. Probert and Doreen Humphry remembered the cricket matches when Winnie Burgess served tea. Rev. Probert organised a clergy cricket team and when the women's team played against the men, the men had to play left handed!

There used to be dances in the old church room when Bert Adams and his wife from Fivehead played the accordion. Nancy Humphry held whist drives in the old church room. There was also a library, held there once a week, run by Miss Chorley and Mrs. Manning and later by Miss Salmon. The council came to change the books.

John Steele recalled pranks in his youth with his friend Bernard Habberfield. John had an old unlicensed motorbike and rode around on Sundays and camped in Mrs Priddle's orchard. There was a pub at Isle Brewers, a simple ciderhouse; they would cross a narrow plank across the river near the weir. They would then tie pieces of couch grass together to trip up others coming home drunk across the fields! Bill Burton, Don Tapp and others went to the pub to play skittles. John also enjoyed visiting the Ilminster Sheep Fair every year. He would go with Bernard Habberfield and walk his father's sheep from Isle Abbots and then enjoy the fairground. He also remembered going to a Mission with Bernard one summer. It was held in a marquee in Church Close for a week. There was singing, Bible talks, treasure hunts etc. He would have been aged about 9-12 at the time.

Brenda Innes remembered playing in Spider Lane with her friends Sheila Priddle and Margaret Squires. Spider Lane is now an overgrown drove, which ran from the junction by Northalls Farm to the fields of Bromes Farm. They would walk miles together and on Sunday summer afternoons walked to a house by the old greenhouses (junction of Cad Road) where an Italian family made ice cream and sold it from their garage. She would also enjoy clotting for eels with her father Harry. They would dig worms and thread them on a long piece of wool and make a ball. This would be tied to a piece of wire on a stick to attract the eels, which they took home to cook. Her father also made them wooden toys, stilts, clowns on sticks, catapults and whistles.

Brenda also recalled skittling for a pig in the old barns opposite Marshes (now three bungalows). Mr. Felton, who ran a pig farm next to Greenhatch provided the pig. At one time dress making classes were held in the school and Brenda made a smocked dress for her baby daughter Charmaine.

The Hunt meets at Northalls Farm 2003, showing the "Back House" before conversion

Hunting and horse riding has always been popular; the hunt would meet at various local farms during the winter.

An annual highlight was a concert. In 1907 a newspaper report in the County Gazette read 'The annual concert, arranged by Misses Barrington (Mary & Sarah) of Northalls, was held in the Council Schoolroom. All artists were in excellent form despite prevailing cold weather. Through the kindness of Mr Samuel Tapp a spacious platform was erected with a backdrop of lace curtains before a large and appreciative audience. Mr. Matterson of Langport, Mr. Templeman of Hambridge and Mr. Vine of Ilminster provided humorous portions. The whole concert raised 11 guineas for the benefit of Taunton and Somerset Hospital.'

Another report reads 'In Feb. 1904 a Temperance entertainment was given in the Baptist schoolroom. Mr. S. Tapp presided. Miss Adams, who had taught the children some pretty songs, presided at the organ. The program included two songs by Mrs. James Slade, addresses by Mr. Sidney Slade, four recitations and four songs by the Band of Hope children. Several pledges were taken at the close.'

THE VILLAGE CHOIR

In 2001 a community choir was started under the leadership of David Sutcliffe. Meeting weekly in the village hall, the choir has performed at many events in the village and for special services in the church. They have also sung several times at Stourhead Gardens and many fund raising concerts and

The Village Choir perform at Stourhead Gardens, May 2008

Christmas Carol services in other villages. Initially formed of just village residents, the membership has grown to over 30 people, including visitors from surrounding villages.

CAROL SINGING

For many years from about the 1970s some villagers went around the houses singing carols and collecting money for charities. For several years an active group of youngsters took this on and had great fun until they all left the village and unfortunately the custom has died out for the moment.

Village youngsters singing carols and collecting for charity (Bromes House, 2011)

Happy walkers at Otterford Lakes....

WALKING GROUP

This was formed in 2010 under the leadership of Carolyn Pix and Barbara Rickitt. Meeting monthly, an average of 12 people discover many new walks within a short driving distance of the village. The occasional teashop or pub lunch all add to the fun.

....and Near Montacute (both taken 2013)

BOOK CLUB

A newly formed book club began in 2008. Meeting in people's houses, a wide range of books have been read and discussed.

Raising funds for the Playgroup on the Railway, 2013

RAILWAY

Work on the private 7¼-inch gauge Isle Abbots railway started in 2000. It was the brainchild of Martin Rickitt and was originally planned as a short length of track. It has grown over the years to well over half a mile including a tunnel and a station at the rear of the Village Hall. The railway sees good use with fund raising events for various village organisations. A variety of steam, electric and petrol driven locomotives, together with various passenger carriages and goods wagons are available to run on the railway. A major event in the railway calendar is the "Santa Special day" held each year in aid of village fund-raising.

Most other forms of recreation today now centre on church and village hall events.

Emily Colenso and Granddad with children Ross and Ella fishing for tadpoles at Cox's Pit, summer 2002

~~~ The Friendship Club ~~~

The Women's voluntary Service established friendship Clubs throughout England in 1938. Their object was to provide facilities for recreation and leisure time occupation to improve the condition of the lives of pensioners and to organise, make and receive suggestions for both indoor and outdoor activities to benefit club members.

Mrs. M. Wigfield, WRVS Centre Organiser for Langport Rural District Council, called a public meeting in Isle Abbots village hall on 4th April 1968. This was to establish if anyone would like to start a club for the over 60s in the village. This idea was received with enthusiasm by the 18 or so people present and a committee formed of Mrs. Wigfield (WRVS Organiser), Mrs, Freer (Chairman), Miss Vincent (Vice Chairman), Miss Staniforth (Secretary), Mrs. Pickford (Treasurer) and Mrs. Harry Adams.

At their first meeting in May 1968 the name of 'Friendship Club' was adopted and suggestions for monthly meetings discussed. The District Council gave a grant and the clubs own fund raising activities would support the meetings. It was agreed that the club need not be restricted to the over 60's and that people from outside the village could attend. The cost for hiring the village hall was 7s 6d and tea and biscuits were served. Everyone paid 3d (or more) towards the expenses.

Over the years a wide variety of speakers came to the village covering an amazing amount of subjects, bird watching, photography, furs, beautiful Britain by bicycle, bees, accident prevention, a dietician about 'food on a pension', gardens in retirement, Nigeria, the growth of music halls. Also numerous slide shows of members' holidays abroad, films by Guide Dogs for the Blind and even one on the introduction of decimal currency.

In 1968 the Chief Public Health Inspector for the Rural District Council spoke to the meeting about a unified sewerage system being prepared linking the 26 villages into 5 districts each with a disposal plant. He answered questions about flooding, clearing ditches and road repairs. Members asked when Isle Abbots would benefit from the ambitious drainage scheme. He said it was hoped to link Isle Abbots with the new drain being laid at Fivehead. (Note: this eventually came about 30 years later!)

By October 1968 there were 41 members. Their first Christmas party held that year was reported as a great success "the village hall looked very gay with decorations and a lighted Christmas tree". There was a raffle when Mrs Habberfield won a teddy bear. An excellent meal was provided of cold ham, tongue, salad, pickles, bread and butter, jellies, mince pies, Christmas cake, cups of tea and sherry. Three groups from Fivehead provided entertainment and the evening ended with the singing of "Auld Lang Syne".

The club also went on many outings over the years. These were very popular as not many members had their own cars. Coaches were hired for visits to Lynmouth and Exmoor, Dunster and Minehead, Cricket St Thomas, East Lambrook Gardens, Weston Super Mare for Norbury's Knitwear Fashion Show, Swanage amongst many others.

There were many tea parties, bazaars and Christmas parties with local entertainment, mainly from talented people within the group. Games were played such as dominoes, cards, bingo, dumb charades, musical games and judging from the Minute book, everybody had a lot of fun. There is no doubt that the Club provided much friendship and enlightenment for the older villagers.

In 1969 Mrs. Joan Crisp took over as Chairman from Mrs Freer who had sold her home, 'The Old School House', and would be leaving the village. Mrs Crisp said, "the club could not ask anyone to come and sing to us because the piano is so dreadful". A replacement Chappell piano was acquired from Curry Mallet for £5 and £3 was paid to the removal man.

Two of the more amusing moments taken from the minutes, was that in 1970 Mr. Bicknell reported that the Club's stock of Horlicks was low and that Mrs. Withers offered to purchase a large carton of one pound jars at

Crewkerne Cash & Carry for Welfare. At the next meeting it was reported that the consignment had been purchased along with a case of Marmite.

It was recorded that in 1971 there were 45 members but from that year on the numbers began to dwindle and in 1977 at the AGM it was reported that many members had died or moved away. Although the club continued for many years there are no minutes to mark later gatherings.

Berkeley Johnson, the Chapel Minister took over from Mrs Crisp in the early 1980s and continued until he moved away, and no-one could be found to continue running the Club. By this time some members had their own cars and could access other forms of entertainment. Many transferred to the existing club at Fivehead.

Friendship Club meeting at Cuffs Orchard, 1973

Joan Crisp, Berkeley and Alice Johnson at Sidmouth.

~~~ The Village Hall ~~~

The earliest mention of a possible village hall was made at the Parish Council meeting in 1947 when Mr. Wood reported on the work of his sub-committee. "Although two suitable sites had been found and terms arranged with the landlords, the cost of erecting, equipping and maintaining a hut was too great to entertain at the present time." An alternative suggestion was made that the church council be asked to place the church room at the disposal of the village and after considerable controversy and discussion the chairman was asked to approach the vicar.

Official Opening of the Village Hall, July 1982.
Sqn Ldr John Steele, Col John Stevens (Jt. Chairmen), Coun Penelope Phillips
Barbara Rickitt (Secretary), Audrey Smith-West (Catering)

In 1959 the County Education Committee offered the redundant school for a village hall for £1 per annum rent with the village paying the maintenance.

THE VILLAGE HALL *written by George Withers.*

To the tune of "Did You Ever See?"
Sung with a mock Welsh accent, as sung by Max Boyce

They said we had no hope at all to restore our Village Hall
"Before you get your new extension, boyo, you'll get your old age pension"
Did you ever see, did you ever see, did you ever see such a funny thing before?

Well it seemed a dreadful pity, so we formed a new committee
And we started raising money, just like bees collecting honey.
Did you ever see……

Well you know the gallant Colonel (*John Stevens*) he kept us on our toes eternally,
As chairman of a meetin' he will take a bit of beatin'
Did you ever see……

Playground wall was none too clever, had no future, none whatever
And the hole was soon made bigger by our Tony (*Habberfield*) with his digger.
Did you ever see……

Well, the builders worked like ants, busy spendin' all our grants
But now the kitchen's standing there, with new tables and new chairs.
Did you ever see……

There's my wife, I can't restrain her since she saw that double drainer.
"They should look at my old kitchen" Will she never stop her bitching?
Did you ever see……

Village picnic by the Isle made the population smile
In a boat with Richard (*Burgess*) rowin, there's no knowin' where you're goin'
Did you ever see……

Got a girl named Valerie, Ballet Dance Academy (*Dresser*)
If you're ever passing through, you should see her Pas de Deux.
Did you ever see……

Looking' back, it seems amazin' how we did that money raisin'
But we put our shoulders to it, and we showed them we could do it.
Did you ever see……

A referendum was held with 78 in favour and 7 against. In 1961 an existing Village Trust Fund was transferred to the Village Hall Committee.

In 1978 another referendum and lively discussion was held and parishioners voted by a large majority to buy the hall from the Council for £2,600 of which £625 must come directly from the village.

There were great activities to raise funds to purchase the old school. Mrs. Renée Bicknell put up the money for a guarantee and the Handkerchief Tree in the old playground was planted in her memory. Joint Chairmen Sqn. Ldr. John Steele and Colonel John Stevens headed the committee. Randal Davis was Treasurer and Nancy Langmaid Secretary, followed in 1979 by Barbara Rickitt. For several years there was a constant program of entertainment to raise funds to equip the hall and build a new kitchen and indoor toilets to replace the outside privies used by the school. Audrey Smith-West organised most of the catering for events, often providing quantities of her home made wine. With a grant from Yeovil District Council the Hall was officially purchased in 1980 and the new extension of kitchen, storeroom and cloakrooms had been completed by November that year.

Villagers willingly joined in the entertainment and hidden talents were brought out with singing and sketches. George Withers was one of the main organisers of such events. George was well known for singing folk songs and often re-wrote traditional songs to bring in local events and names and his sister Marjorie would often accompany him on the piano.

The Village Picnic, 1979: Richard Burgess rowing Susan Vickery with Catherine, Emma and Martha

Christmas Party, 1979: Children Entertain
Catherine Vickery, Tracey Hardwill, Rachel Rickitt, Alison and Andrew Humphry, Paul Adams, Mark Dresser, Michael Adams, Richard Rickitt, Emma Vickery, Lou and Kenny Hardwill

In July 1982 Councillor Penelope Phillips, Chairman of Somerset County Council, officially opened the improved hall

With improvement provided by grants and village events the Village Hall has seen constant use since it opened, providing a centre for village social life and a home for the Playgroup.

In 2004 a marquee was kindly donated to the village hall in memory of Sq. Ldr. John Steele, thus continuing the good work he helped to start. This has been a great asset and is used for larger events such as balls and shows when more space is needed and is erected with kind permission of landowners, usually Anthony Habberfield at Northalls Farm, or John Medcalf behind his house Thimble Hall.

Fancy Dress at the Victorian Picnic: *Emma, Martha, William & Catherine Vickery*

1980: Victorian Picnic by the Isle:
George Withers falls in, helped out by Richard Humphry

Tug of War - Village picnic 1979:
Mervyn Vickery, Reg. Burgess, Geoff Miller, Bernard Adams, John Humphry >< Martin Rickitt, John Lucas (and others!)

Victorian Picnic by River Isle 1980
Barbara Rickitt, Wendy Richards and Alistair

1981 Christmas Party: *Snow White, produced by Val Dresser*
Alison Humphry as Prince, Samantha Dresser as Snow White

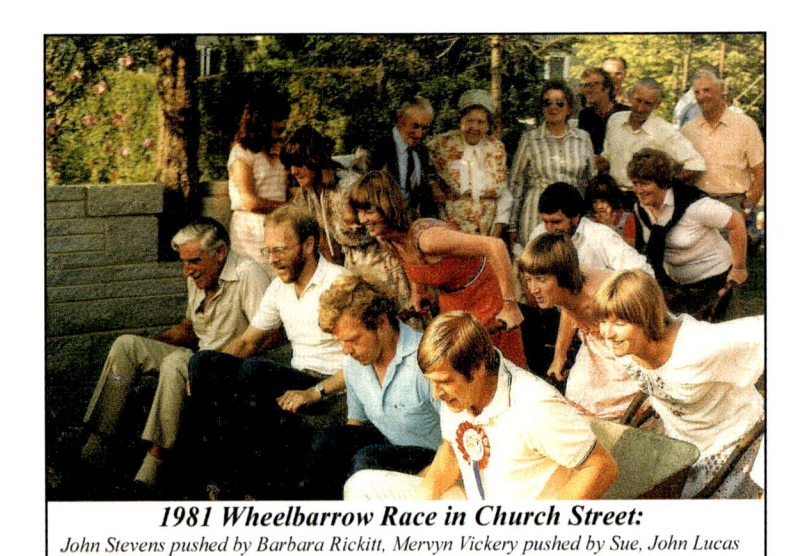

1981 Village Christmas Party:
The keep fit class entertain: Vicky Miller & Di Lucas at front

1981 Wheelbarrow Race in Church Street:
John Stevens pushed by Barbara Rickitt, Mervyn Vickery pushed by Sue, John Lucas pushed by Diane; Geoff Miller pushed by Vicky. Bernard & Sonia Adams behind.

1986 Christmas Party:
George Withers, Alan Weller, Richard Burgess, John Stevens, Richard Humphry, John Steele

1980: Building the new kitchen and toilets

The School "Privy"- 2 cubicles, 4 seats: 1975- This stood in the Village Hall garden

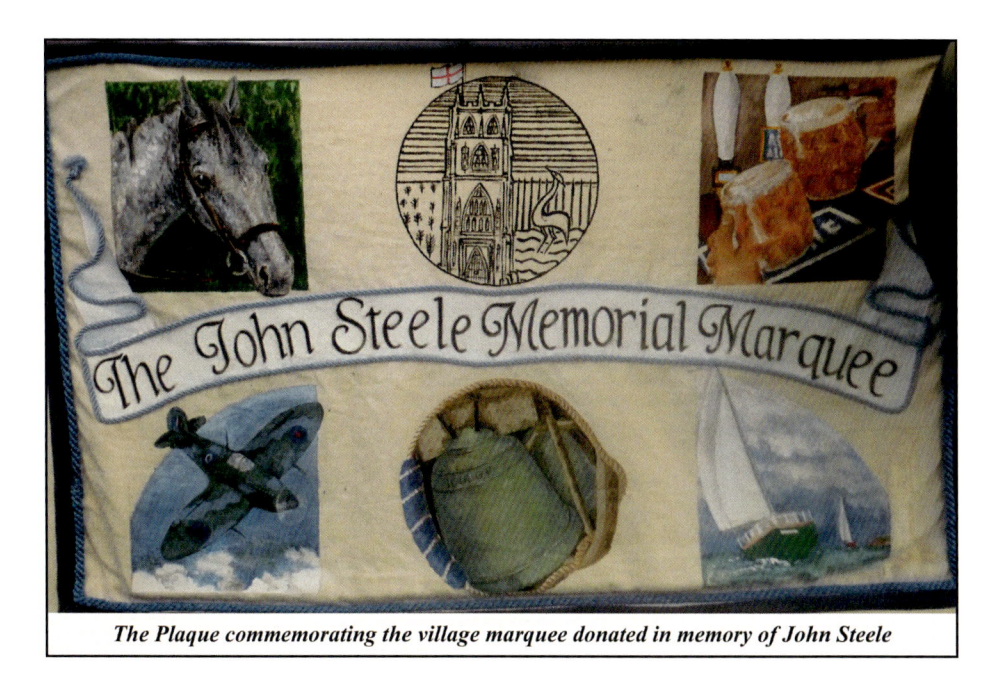

The Plaque commemorating the village marquee donated in memory of John Steele

Jubilee Show 2002: Uncle Tom Cobley: Organised by the Village Hall Committee in the Marquee
Mark Humphry, Brian Cleal, Martin Rickitt, [hidden], Tony Habberfield, Mike Smith

Carribean Beach Party, 2002
Mervyn Vickery, Peter Watts and Diane Lucas

Carribean Beach Party 2002:
Sue Vickery with Hula Hoop

2003: Start of the Easter Morning Duck Race

The 2007 Review: The Pop Group-
*Peter Cottell, Robbie Robson, Peter Watts
backed by Barbara Rickitt and Elaine Guest*

Old Folks Christmas Lunch, 2008:
L to R: Kath & Dave Phillimore, Sheila Simpson, Evelyn Stevens, Frances Burgess
Joan Lawrence, Avril & George Withers, served by Peter Watts

St George's Day Lunch 2012:
Kath Phillimore, Lesley Sutcliffe, Jane Oakley & Margaret Massman

Harvest Supper, 2013
Sheila Simpson & Doreen Humphry

Village Coffee Morning, December 2014:
Robbie Robson, Bob Pix, Martin Rickitt, John Medcalf

~~~ Employment Overview ~~~

The biggest source of employment over the years has been farming and the related trades mentioned under other chapters. But when people began to get cars it was possible to live in the village and work some distance away. This starts to show when the baptismal registers gave the trade of the child's father, and becomes more evident from the 1950s onwards.

Apart from domestic work, a major source of employment for women at home was glove making. The materials would be delivered to the house and the finished gloves collected. Other home employment was making collars, shirts and stays.

In the late 19th and early 20th Century Tapps agricultural machinist based at Colliers would have employed many men and the demand for supplying and repairing agricultural equipment would have been great.

The village bakery, shop and post office provided employment for a few. Local builders, carpenters and thatchers would have been busy, not forgetting the gravedigger and travelling trades people from surrounding villages. The cordwainer (shoemaker) was mentioned nine times in the registers.

Brenda Innes (nee Adams) remembered her mother Lily making gloves, selling rabbits caught with ferrets, and cutting teasels by the river Rag (Fivehead River).

Ethel Paterson (nee Wilcox) recalled when she used to pick Blackberries with her cousin Kit. These were sold to a man for 2d a pound. They were put in a big barrel and she thought they might have been used for dye. *Frances Burgess* also remembered picking Blackberries for sale.

John Steele remembered when Mr Akers, who at one time lived at Greenhatch, used to repair hearses in a shed up Iberry Lane. Jack Willy was a lengthman for the County Council and had a donkey and trap. The donkey was buried under the walnut tree at Colliers. Noah Hopkins had a 3-wheeled bike with a shovel and pick tied to it, and kept the Isle Brewers road. Jo Sealey also worked on the roads.

At one time Polly Adams delivered the post. She collected it from Fivehead and delivered right round to Bradon. When she retired John Steele, as Parish Meeting Chairman, presented her with a standard lamp from the village.

John and Paul Matravers used the forge at the side of Colliers for shoeing horses and for other metal work for many years before they expanded to premises at Roundoak and Fivehead.

In the mid 20th century chicken rearing sheds were built at Steamalong adjacent to Greenhatch.

Now in the 21st century, far fewer people are employed on the farms. With the exception of the three major farms, nearly everyone in the village owns a cars and goes elsewhere for work. With the aid of computers and modern communications some people are once again able to be home workers.

Teasel growing used to be a major source of employment in the area. Wild teasels, like these by the Fivehead River, are still seen as a reminder of those times.

FLOODING of the surrounding fields has been a feature of village life since the earliest times, as Isle Abbots lies near the confluence of the River Isle and the Fivehead River. Fortunately this rarely affects properties. These two pictures were taken from the Church Tower in November 2012.

Right: Looking North along Otterham Lane towards the Fivehead River and Fivehead village.

Below: Looking South towards Bradon and Puckington.

~~~ Bibliography and Acknowledgements ~~~

Books and documents referred to:-

Isle Abbots by Elizabeth Bicknell, c.1970
The History & Antiquities of Somerset, John Collinson (1791)
Pevsner
The Church Builder 1908
Elizabeth Bicknell's Scrapbook
Parish Council Minutes
St Mary the Virgin, Parochial Church Council Minutes, Faculties and other old documents
Mrs Woods "little black book"
Isle Abbots Friendship Club Minutes
Somerset County Gazette
History booklet about the Baptist Chapel

Interviews made with a future book specifically in mind; some people also provided photographs:-

† = now deceased

Jack Adams †
Frances Burgess †
Joan Crisp †
Doreen Humphry
Anthony Habberfield
John & Nancy† Humphry
Betty & Joan Hurford †
Brenda Innes †
Dick Lucas
Ethel Patterson †
Violet Priddle †
Mrs S Probert †
Sqn. Ldr. John Steele †
Phyllis Tapp
George† and Avril† Withers

~~~~~~

Other people who have given me helpful information over the years, and in some cases provided pictures.

Richard Burgess
Betty Cropper (North Curry Archives)
Edmund Dare
Helen & Danny Evans
Peter Herbert
Mark Humphry
John & Diane Lucas
Barbara Painter
Bob & Jacqueline Patten
Wendy Richards
Betty Sheale
David Sutcliffe
Susan & Mervyn Vickery
Somerset Records Office
David Bradshaw and Bob Pix for help with design
Andrew Sweeting for the cover photograph
Gary Smith for A2 scanning

Also thanks to those from whom I have gleaned information during a casual conversation.

The Village website: **www.isle-abbotts.org.uk** has been a source of information and illustrations and is updated with current events and happenings in the village.